THE
CREDIT
IMPROVEMENT
AND
PROTECTION
HANDBOOK

OSCAR RODRIGUEZ

J. FLORES
PUBLICATIONS
P.O. BOX 830131
MIAMI, FL 33283-0131

This book is available in ELECTRONIC BOOK computer disk version in IBM compatible format.

To order an electronic version of this book send check or credit card information (card number and expiration date) for $19.95 plus $3 S&H. to:

J. Flores Publications
P.O. Box 830131
Miami, FL 33283-0131

For Faster Service call Toll Free **1-800-472-2388**, anytime. (Credit card orders only).

Please specify title of book and disk size. (3.5" or 5.25" disk.)

THE CREDIT IMPROVEMENT AND PROTECTION HANDBOOK by Oscar Rodriguez

Copyright © 1993 by Oscar Rodriguez

Published by:
J. Flores Publications
P.O. Box 830131
Miami, FL 33283-0131

Direct inquires and/or order to the above address.

ISBN 0-918751-32-2

Library of Congress Catalog Card Number: 93-70051

Printed in the United States of America

DEDICATION

This book is dedicated to the over 100 million Americans who today have derogatory information as part of their credit record, and the need to participate in this credit-oriented society, but are not allowed to. **The biggest problem with credit is that it doesn't come with an instruction book!** This may have been true, up until now. The key is a set of simple, safe, and proved strategies that you can use immediately to strengthen your financial position, protect yourself and your family, and regain control of your financial destiny. It's the only guide you'll ever need to chart a safe course toward enduring credit and economic success.

– Oscar Rodriguez

FOREWORD

You are not helpless... this book is intended to outline legal methods that you, the consumer, can use to **improve** your credit report. You will also learn what your credit rights are and how to utilize them to your benefit. The negative credit that is now being listed on your file will remain **seven to ten years** unless you do something about it. If you follow this step by step guide, you do not have to be one of those helpless victims always at the mercy of their credit file. You will also find in this book such things as who has information on you and why you should beware. Plus, how you can obtain a MasterCard, Visa or other credit cards with a very liberal credit check. We have spent considerable time and money researching the consumer protection laws and perfecting a system that will save you a great deal of time and effort... one that has helped people from all walks of life with credit problems. After all, being able to obtain credit is no longer a luxury, but rather a necessity; and everything is based on what is contained in your credit file!

The high standards of living enjoyed by millions of Americans today, as well as the lifeblood of our economy, is based upon the extension of credit. Consumers in the past with credit problems have had nowhere to turn for advice, guidance, or a solution to their problem. These consumers are mad and angry, and want to fight back. Credit and credit needs are not only growing, but growing by leaps and bounds. It's importance cannot be over emphasized, and if used wisely, it can fulfill dreams.

The publisher sincerely hopes you take advantage of the procedures and the techniques explained to you in this self help handbook. It's up to you... get started today on your way to AAA Credit!

TABLE OF CONTENTS

INTRODUCTION
    Your Credit History 1
    What to Do if You're Having Problems 1
    Can an Average Person Become Wealthy Just By Saving Money? 2
    How Much Should You Save Each Month? 3

PART ONE: CREDIT REPAIR
    Credit Bureaus 5
    Where Do Credit Bureaus Get Their Information? 5
    What Information Does A Credit Report Contain? 6
    Credit Correction (Step By Step Process) 8
    Negotiating Outstanding Balances 13
    Bankruptcies, Judgments, Liens and Credit Reports 14
    Location of Major Credit Bureaus 14
    Credit Report Request Form 20
    Formal Complaints and the Federal Trade Commission ...21
    Adding Favorable Items To Credit Reports 21
    Multiple Credit Reports 22
    What is an Alternate File? 22
    How Do Alternate Files Occur? 22
    Merging or Piggy-Backing 24
    Sample Dispute Letters 25
    Sample Consumer Statement 28
    Sample Credit Reference Additions Letter 29
    Sample No Response to a Dispute Letter 30
    Sample Letter to Credit Bureau Decoding Department 31
    Illegal Credit Inquiry Letter 32
    Free Publications from the Governors of the Federal Reserve 33
    Federal Reserve Bank Addresses 33
    The Fair Credit Reporting Act 35

PART TWO: CREDIT CARDS AND SETTLEMENT COSTS
    Credit Cards – A General Overview 47
    Tax Reform Act and Credit Card Interest Expense 47
    Fraudulent Credit Card Billings and What To Do 48
    Types of Credit Cards 49
    Banks Aggressively Looking to Issue Credit Cards 51
    Secured Credit Cards 52
    How to Apply for a Credit Card 53
    The Cost of Credit (Buyer Beware) 54
    Valuable Facts About Credit Card Use 55
    Closing Costs (Important Information Needed Before Buying) 55
    How to Obtain a Secured Credit Card 56

TABLE OF CONTENTS, Continued

PART TWO, continued

Use the Bank's Money to Obtain
a Secured Credit Card and Establish Credit 57
Secured Credit Card Sources 58
Lowest Interest Credit Card Sources (With Annual Fees) 58
Lowest Interest Credit Card Sources (No Annual Fees) 61
Multiple Credit Card Acquisitions 62
Consumer Rights Concerning Prompt Crediting & Billing 63
Secured Credit Card Request Form 64
Fair Credit Billing Act 65

PART THREE: ACQUIRING CREDIT

Proper Methods In Establishing Credit 73
How to Get A Car Loan Even if You Are Non-Financable 74
What Creditors Look For 74
Credit Scoring System 75
What Banks Consider To Be Negative Information 77
How to Improve Your Chances Applying for a Loan 78
AAA Credit in Thiry Days 81
Personal Budget Worksheet 83
Loan Request Cover Letter 84
Net Worth Worksheet 85
Debt Service and Financing Worksheet 87
Credit Confirmation Form 88
Women, Minorities and Credit 89
Summary of the Equal Credit Opportunity Act 89
Filing A Complaint If You Have Been Discriminated Against 90
Sample Formal Discrimination Complaint 92
Equal Credit Opportunity Act 93

PART FOUR: CREDIT COLLECTION

Monthly Delinquencies 99
Collection Agencies 100
Fair Debt Collection Practices Act In Summary 100
How to Avoid Collection Problems 102
How to Handle Collection Agencies 102
Bankruptcy: Ch. 13 vs. Ch. 7 103
Debt Relief: Chapter 13, The Wage Earner Plan 104
Bankruptcy: Chapter 7, Total Freedom From Debts 106
Other Legal Strategies 106
Settlement Letter 109
Judgment Proofing (Step by Step Process) 110
Fair Debt Collection Practices Act 113

INTRODUCTION

Your Credit History
Your Second Most Important Financial Asset!

How important is your credit history? Just ask anyone unfortunate enough to end up with a *bad* credit history!

In our credit-oriented society, a person who cannot obtain credit has a very difficult time. I recently sat beside a gentleman on an airliner who is a successful businessman, earning $60,000 a year. However, five years ago, he owned a business which was in trouble, and he developed a credit history of slow and missed payments. As a result, he is unable to obtain credit now, and has to use cash everywhere he goes. In addition, he says he is embarrassed every time he checks into a hotel and tells them he has no credit cards. He gets funny looks and the hotels make him pay cash in advance; then they usually notate his account **"NO CHARGES ALLOWED"**.

The Biggest Problem with Credit is that it Doesn't Come with Instructions!

Lenders look for two things before granting credit:

1) What is the applicant's ability to repay the credit?

2) What is the applicant's willingness to repay the credit? (Your *Credit History!*)

When you are granted credit, your lender reports your payment history monthly to one or more national reporting services. The information stays in your file for seven years. It follows you no matter where you move in the country. We've received credit applications from people who moved from Eastern states, where they had bad credit records, who felt they could apply for credit in a new, Western state where they weren't known. However, all the information from the old state is in the national computer system, and available to any lender in just seconds.

If your records shows a history of slow, or missed payments to previous lenders, most new lenders will reject your credit application because you have exhibited inability, or unwillingness, to pay your bills. Most people **need** credit to finance large purchases such as autos, homes, furniture or entertainment equipment, such as sound systems or camping equipment. Thus, a bad credit history may put all of these things out of a person's reach.

What To Do If You're Having Problems:

1) Lenders realize that most people have temporary cash-flow problems from time to time. If you have a problem, *tell your lenders!* Most lenders will work with you through your period of difficulty. **The worst thing** you can do is to skip payments with no explanation. That indicates and unwillingness to pay, and upsets lenders. At the very least, make partial payments on your past due date, which indicates willingness on your part.

2) Some lenders, such as phone/utility companies and landlords, don't report credit history. Always make sure your **reportable** bills are paid on time, and consider delaying payment of the non-reportable bills.

3) Develop a plan (or budget) for paying your bills.

4) Live within your means. If you can't afford something, don't buy it.

5) Consider the use of a credit-counseling service or a credit correction handbook.

6) **Always** save part of your pay each month so that you build an emergency reserve, which can tide you over during tough times.

By the way, what's your *most* important financial asset? **Your income**, of course. A person earning an *average* of only $20,000 a year will generate $800,000 in earnings, which he/she will control the spending of, over a normal work career.

Remember, responsible people will save a significant portion of their earnings; irresponsible people will spend it all!

Can an Average Person Become Wealthy By Just Saving Money?

The answer is an unqualified *yes!* But, it takes desire, discipline, patience and a knowledge of how **compound interest** works.

Most of the spectacular investment gains from compound interest occur in the second half of any savings period. For example, if a person were to save $100 per month for an entire working career of 40 years, the total savings deposits would be $48,000. If the account were earning an average of 10%, compound interest would build the total value of the account to a whopping $637,678!

However, most of the gain (87%) of $589,678 occurs during the second 20 year period of the investment. This is why so many people fail when it comes to saving money – they lose their patience.

On the chart at the top of the next page, the top line is the growth of the Total Account Value. Notice how flat the curve is in the first 20 years, and then how it grows steeply in the second 20 years, as the total account value increases. Most people save for 3 - 5 years, only accumulate $3,000 to $7,000 and then lose patience and spend the money on a new car or vacation. That's the worst thing to do! By taking the money out of the savings account, just as the shape of the curve is increasing, they are missing out on the steep growth. After they've gotten through the hard part, they "rob" the account (and themselves) and put their savings plan into the flat, slow-growth part of the curve.

Also, watch the interest rate you're earning. For instance, the same deposits above put into a bank savings account at 5 1/2% interest would only be worth $174,903 – a difference of $462,775 **less** earnings in our saver's pocket!

SAVING $100/MONTH AT 10% INTEREST

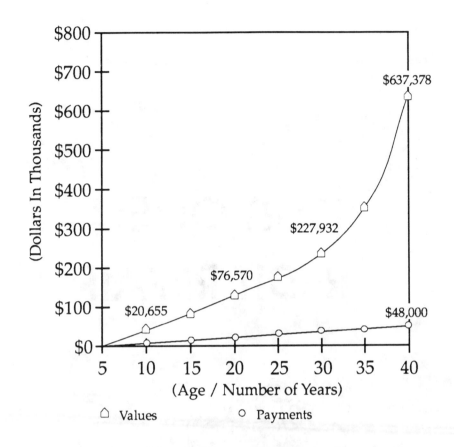

How Much Should You Save Each Month?

Most financial planners agree that you should save a minimum of 10% of your pay each month, if you are ever to become financially independent. (The average worker's savings rate is 16% in Japan and 13% in West Germany) Most planners also agree that the best way to save money is to find a way to cut the waste out of your budget. Most people waste $100-$300 per month on junk food and other frivolous expenditures, and then wonder where all their money went at the end of the month. All planners agree that if you are to be successful, you must **pay yourself first** each month by paying your savings deposit before any other payments are made.

PART ONE:
CREDIT REPAIR

PART ONE: CREDIT REPAIR

The following are simple, safe and proven strategies that you can use immediately to strengthen your financial position, protect yourself and your family, and regain control of your financial destiny.

Credit Bureaus

A credit bureau is a central clearing house of credit information. There are five major credit bureaus (TRW, CBI, Trans-Union, Chilton, and Associated Credit – See maps later in this section for areas) and hundreds of small local bureaus. **All bureaus do not contain the same information** or all of a consumer's credit history.

Where Do Credit Bureaus Get Their Information?

Lending institutions subscribe to credit bureaus in order to ascertain the credit and payment history of a potential applicant. In turn (and in many instances for a discount on their subscription rate), **some** (not all) **lending institutions report their credit experience to the bureau**, who, in turn, process this information and add it to the consumer's credit file/report. Credit bureaus do not give the consumer a credit rating per se: credit bureaus report the information given to them by its subscribers. It is, therefore, possible for a bureau to report obsolete, erroneous, incomplete, inaccurate, outdated and/or misleading information and not be aware of it. Lending institutions grant credit based on their own in-house underwriting policies, part of which is based on the information contained in a credit report. It is also important to know that many employers will "pull" (run) a credit report on a job applicant to evaluate him/her. All consumers should have their reports updated, corrected and changed if necessary, even if presently they feel they have no need to do so.

Most consumers are unaware of how much credit information is **not** included in their report. The following is a list of items and institutions who usually **do NOT report to the credit bureaus.** They are classified as limited subscribers, since they only inquire as to someone's credit files and do not input their credit experience with their clients. They are usually:

- Small Banks
- Home Mortgages (Savings & Loans)
- Utility Companies
- Oil Companies
- American Express

- Small/Medium Credit Unions
- Rent Payments
- Medical Bills
- Savings or Checking Account Information
- Insurance Companies

Even though a financial institution may choose not to report (input) the consumer's payment history (unless he/she defaults; then many of them through their third party collection agency retained to collect the account may report the impropriety); they do, however, run credit reports on the applicant prior to extending them credit initially.

The following is a list of financial institutions that usually **DO report to credit bureaus.** They are classified as Automatic Subscribers since they report their credit experience automatically every month to the bureaus, in addition to inquiring into the consumer's credit report prior to granting him credit. The incentive given to Automatic Subscribers by bureaus to report every month is usually a discount on the cost of pulling (running) credit reports.

These institutions usually report to credit bureaus:

- Major Banks
- Major Department Stores
- Travel and Entertainment Cards
- Finance/Loan Companies
- Major Savings & Loans;
- Collection Agencies
  Consumer Loan Departments
  (Car loans, credit cards, etc.)

In addition to the above, credit bureaus also get information from public courthouse records (for example: judgements, bankruptcy filings, liens, wage garnishments, Chapter 13 Wage Earner Plans, etc.).

What Information Does A Credit Report Contain?

A credit report is basically composed in the following fashion:

1. Identification

Because of the tremendous number of files contained in a credit bureau computer (with all the credit bureaus combined, there is virtually a credit file on almost every adult resident of the United States), and the possibility of similar names, addresses, or mistaken social security numbers; credit bureaus will identify consumers by complete name, address (previous address, if less than two years at present address), social security number, and date of birth. Some credit bureaus will also permit subscribers to input information regarding the consumer's employment, salary and number of years at his present employment.

2. Credit Inquiries

Every time a subscriber runs a credit report on a consumer, the computer automatically records this inquiry. This inquiry will remain on the consumer's report for a period of approximately 12 months (Illinois, Oregon and Texas for two years). **These inquiries are of interest to creditors because it gives them an idea of the applicant's recent credit dealings.**

3. Public Records and Collection Accounts

As previously explained, credit bureaus have access to public records from courthouse records. Additionally, when a creditor gives an uncollectible to a collection agency, the agency will generally report this to the credit bureau.

4. Credit History

The name and identification number of each reporting subscriber, along with the consumer's history (example – how many times was he 30 days, 60 days, 90 days, or more late); the date the account was opened, original balance or high credit limit, original terms, current balance, monthly payment amount, and the date of last subscriber input is contained on his credit history. Any irregularity or important information in a consumer's account can also be listed, such as the following:

a) **Consumer Dispute**	Consumer is disputing a charge on his credit card which he feels he is not liable for.
b) **Criminal Conviction**	Includes records of arrest and indictments from date of release for seven years.
c) **Individual Liability**	Is the consumer the only person liable (responsible for payment) for this account?
d) **Joint Account**	The consumer has a contractual responsibility for this account along with someone else.
e) **Co-Maker**	The consumer has guaranteed payment on this account and should the maker default, the consumer is responsible.
f) **Charge Offs**	A creditor (subscriber) has reported the unpaid balance as a loss.
g) **Secured Account**	Some form of collateral (object of value has been pledged as security in order to procure this loan.
h) **Account/Packet Number**	The account number the creditor has designated to this customer or loan.

5. Consumer Statement

Most consumers are unaware that they have the right to put a statement up to 100 words regarding any item(s) they wish to clarify on their credit report (consumer side of the story). This statement is an important part of the credit correction system.

Credit bureaus like to abbreviate on credit reports as often as possible. If they are able to transmit the same amount of information with fewer words and/or characters, they are saving computer time, paper, and other expenses associated with their business function. Each credit bureau has their own reporting style, abbreviations, characters and formats.

Credit Correcting
Step by Step Process

FIRST: The first step in correcting a credit report is to find out exactly which credit bureau(s) are used by lending institutions in the consumer's area. This can be accomplished by looking at the nationwide maps (located in this section of the manual) to determine which of the five major credit bureaus you are located in. Next, contact them by phone requesting the address of their closest branch office. Lastly, by use of the credit report request form, write them to obtain a copy of your credit file. (Remember, there are literally hundreds of small credit bureaus nationwide & requests can only be made in writing.)

Now that we have targeted the bureau(s), we move to the second step.

SECOND: It is impossible to make any credit corrections unless you know exactly what is contained in the credit report. Therefore, you should request a copy. Make sure you use the credit request form found in this section, bureaus need the information requested on it in order to make sure they send the consumer the correct credit report. If the consumer has been turned down or denied credit in the past thirty days, he is entitled to receive his credit report for free. (Always include a photocopy of your credit denial; lenders must provide you with one in order to comply with federal law). If the consumer has not been denied credit in the past thirty days, he will have to pay a modest fee ($5 to $15). The consumer also has the option to go in person to the credit bureau and pick up his report. He should not get involved in an argument or discussion with the clerk regarding the content of the report.

Once the consumer has received his credit report, he should make sure he fully understands it. As previously discussed, all credit bureaus have their own method or system of abbreviating information on a credit report. It is therefore imperative that the consumer learn how to read and fully understand his credit report. Credit bureaus will provide the consumer answers to any question or item he does not fully understand regarding their reporting format. **Since all credit bureaus have their own format and there are hundreds and thousands of credit bureaus, it is impossible and counterproductive to accurately try to teach all of them.** On the back of most credit reports, there are sample credit history files with explanations of their codes. Study them first and then refer to them while reading your file.

THIRD: Once the consumer receives his credit report and fully understands its content, he should write down any item he disagrees with on paper. He should start with his name, address, prior address, date of birth, social security number, employment, previous employment and any other personal item.

Next, he should look at the credit inquiries. As previously discussed, each time a credit report is run by a subscriber, it is automatically recorded on the credit report. **No one may run a credit report on a consumer unless the consumer authorizes it.** The consumer should not want lots of credit inquiries on his report. If a creditor sees a lot of activity on a file, he will begin to wonder why the consumer has been turned down so many times or why his sudden interest in so much credit; it may make the creditor uneasy.

Each time a consumer applies for credit and is rejected, the creditor must advise you why and which credit bureau they used. This written rejection notice permits the consumer, as previously discussed, to get free credit reports. Remember, if you are questioning a credit refusal made within the past 30 days, the bureau is not allowed to charge a fee.

Next, the consumer should look at his payment history, writing down any item appearing with which he disagrees.

All derogatory items after a specific period of time must automatically be removed:

- Bankruptcies: ten (10) years from date of bankruptcy

- All other derogatory items including liens, judgments, late payments, charge offs, repossessions and convictions must be removed after seven (7) years.

Most credit bureaus have their computers automatically programmed to remove these items a few months prior to their anniversary date.

Few creditors, not to mention consumers, are aware that credit bureaus may report your entire credit file since its inception (including all negative information) to a requesting subscriber if the subscriber is involved in granting the consumer any of the following:

- Credit transactions involving $50,000 or more

- Life insurance with a $50,000 value or more

- A consumer applying for a job with a salary of $20,000 or more

FOURTH: The next step is to send the credit bureau a format letter (several samples for reference purpose only are enclosed). The consumer should state all items he disagrees with (and why) and wants investigated. He should state that "these inaccuracies are highly injurious to my credit rating"; **"injurious" is a key word.** The letter should also contain a request for an updated copy of the credit report once the investigation has been completed.

When writing a credit bureau, always write neatly (type if possible), clearly and directly to the point. **Never use foul language, make threats, or** go into personal stories. Always try to document your requests for investigation with copies of checks, bills, notes, or any other type of proof you may have available.

Credit bureaus are required to investigate or re-investigate all items the consumer disputes on his credit report. The Fair Credit Reporting Act does clearly state that credit bureaus do not have to honor a request if the credit bureau feels the request is "frivolous or irrelevant". Credit bureaus in actuality, however, seldom do so. The Federal Trade Commission (governmental agency responsible for overseeing The Fair Credit Reporting Act) has advised credit bureaus not to use this as an excuse in order not to have to investigate reports unless they are prepared to defend their refusal in court.

Once the credit bureau receives the consumer's letter, they have a reasonable amount of time (usually 4 - 6 weeks) to verify the validity of the disputed information with the original reporting subscriber. Remember: **all information added or deleted from a credit report can only be done by the subscriber (creditor);** credit bureaus only report what they are told by the subscriber.

When sending any letter to the credit bureau, the consumer should start a file and keep copies of all correspondence and write notes of any conversations.

If, after a few weeks, the consumer has not received a response from the credit bureau, he should send them a letter inquiring why there has been no response (sample for reference purposes only is enclosed). Make sure you send a copy of the original letter with your inquiry, which should be sent by certified mail on this next occasion. You may also want to follow up with a phone call.

FIFTH: When the consumer finally receives his updated (investigated) credit report, he should compare it with his initial report. On an average, about 50% of the disputed items will have been eliminated. Some credit bureaus will put "no response" if the subscriber did not respond to the credit bureau's request for verification of the disputed item. Why were some items removed and others not? Simple: credit bureaus must verify the disputed information with the subscriber. The subscriber, in many instances, will not bother to respond to the credit bureau's request. The subscriber may not have the personnel available to fulfill the request, they may verify it without checking their records, or they may review their records and find the information is or is not accurate (If an institution only keeps records for 24 months after the transaction has been terminated, how can they verify a late payment if the request for verification comes on the 25th month?).

The next step is to "weed out" the subscribers who are accurately reviewing their records and those who are not.

The next letter to the credit bureau should ask them to re-investigate the items which you are still disputing and why;. A sample letter for reference purposes only is enclosed.

The consumer should state briefly why he feels these items are still showing incorrectly on his credit report.

In this letter it is also wise to **request the company names, address and phone numbers of the subscriber with whom the credit bureau is verifying the disputed inaccuracies.** In this fashion, the consumer can follow up if the disputed inaccuracies are not removed.

This step, which we have just described is how many professional credit repair services **remove negative items from credit reports – true or not!** The credit repair services will send the credit bureau letters **denying everything derogatory including bankruptcy and foreclosures** knowing about 50% of all items will be removed because of the reasons previously stated. They will continue to blitz the credit bureaus with requests for re-investigations until the credit bureau or the subscriber fails to comply in the allotted time. The best month of the year is December because of the holidays.

SIXTH: If after completing the first five steps, there are still items the consumer still wishes to remove, it is time for him to contact the subscriber directly. If possible, this should be done **in person;** however, always make an appointment beforehand. this will assure that the subscriber is available and will also demonstrate to the subscriber that you are driving there to see them exclusively to try to resolve the dispute. Only meet with a credit manager or someone in a position of authority who has the decision-making ability to negotiate the debt.

There are three key words to remember at all times when dealing with a subscriber: **Negotiate! Negotiate! Negotiate!** As with credit bureaus, regardless of what the subscriber says or does, the consumer should never get mad, make threats, or use foul language.

If the discrepancy happened in the past and the consumer's payment history since then has been good, the subscriber may feel compelled not to continue showing this low period in the consumer's payment history (especially if the consumer is a good patron). **The subscriber does not necessarily have to write the bureau a letter to reclarify their new position on the discrepancy. The subscriber can simply not respond to the request for verification by the credit bureau, which, of course, is prompted by the consumer's new request for re-investigation.** This is as previously discussed, will result in the deletion of the discrepancy!

This technique also works very well with credit inquiries. If a credit bureau refuses to investigate or remove inquiries, the consumer should write a letter to the credit bureau's decoding department (sample enclosed for reference purposes only) requesting the name, address and phone number of the subscriber who ran the unauthorized credit reports the consumer is disputing. The consumer should contact the subscriber and explain to them that he never authorized them to run a credit report on him and remind them that they have violated the law.

Unauthorized credit inquiries are a very common problem at car, boat and R.V. dealerships. In many instances, an unsuspecting consumer goes to one of these dealerships that have the practice of sending their credit application to several banks or finance companies all at once for financing. The end result is several inquiries on the consumer's credit report whether he buys or not.

If an account in unpaid and is being shown very unfavorably, what many professional credit correction agencies have advised their clients to do is **offer the creditor payment in full for any outstanding balance only if the subscriber removes the entry from the consumer's report.** Note, this is different from showing an open account that was finally paid. This technique irritates many credit bureaus; they feel it is unethical because accurate information is being deleted from a credit report. Nevertheless, this technique can successfully be accomplished, providing you follow a few important steps. These are discussed in detail under the next heading, "Negotiating Outstanding Balances".

SEVENTH: If, after completing all that has been explained up to now, there still remains some item on the consumer's credit report he feels is not accurately representative of "what really happened", then the consumer has the right to add to his credit report a statement (up to 100 words) presenting his side of the story (see enclosed sample letter for reference purposes only).

Negotiating Outstanding Balances

We would like to point out that all customers of a creditor have a **legal** and **moral** obligation to pay any and all debts they have incurred. When you are dealing with a collection department and/or a collection agency there are some things you want to consider.

First of all, if you have an account that is charged off or turned over to a collection agency, paying the full balance to them will not simply improve that particular account. Most of the time the creditor will just report it from a negative charge off to a negative paid charge off or paid collection. However it is reported, this will still be a derogatory item on your credit file unless you are assured that it will be removed by the creditor or collection agency.

You first want to make contact with the credit department handling your account and explain the situation surrounding the account to them and offer to settle the account if they will remove it and give you this agreement in writing. I cannot express the importance of getting all agreements **in writing.** This will assure that the creditor will delete the item from your file. If they refuse, be persistent. Keep in contact with everyone you speak to or communicate with. You will eventually reach a person who will have the authority or motivation to get the matter settled.

If the creditor will not agree to remove the item, even with payment, write a letter to both the local and national office expressing your desire to pay the bill if they will only remove it from your file. They do, and will, remove these listings if you are persistent in your request. Remember, they want their money more than they want to leave a negative on your file. If they ask for payment and say that upon receipt they will send the requested deletion letter, refuse. This is a trick. Once they cash your check they will deny any knowledge of this "verbal" agreement.

After reaching an agreement, wait for the letter of approval and then make **prompt** payment to the creditor. Don't wait weeks to pay since the creditor will get upset and not honor the agreement for failure to comply. Make sure you live up to any and all agreements you make in regards to settling your account.

The next step is to wait the amount of time the creditor indicated it would take to delete this item and then order a new credit report from your credit reporting agency to make sure the item has been deleted. If it has not been changed, immediately contact the creditor and explain the situation. Usually, they have not gotten around to doing it yet. If they refuse to do it now, you should immediately file a complaint with your state Bureau of Collections and Investigative Services, State Department of Consumer Affairs. In your communication, make sure you include a copy of the agreement and a copy of your most recent credit report. Also send the creditor a copy of the complaint you are filing.

We have included a sample letter to send the creditor to request a deletion along with other sample information that is important in settling your account.

Bankruptcies, Judgments, Liens and Credit Reports

Most credit bureaus obtain or transcribe bankruptcy information directly from public records in the courthouse. Generally this process is done manually by individuals who are paid a modest hourly wage, in many cases are overworked, under staffed and are under pressure to produce. This will undoubtedly lead to the tremendous possibility of inaccuracies being inadvertently reported in the consumer's credit report (bankruptcy dates, bankruptcy amount, etc.)

Depending on which bureau and part of the country, it is estimated that approximately up to 75% of all bankruptcies are being inaccurately reported. If a bankruptcy inaccuracy exists in a consumer's credit report (look closely; the odds are very good there is one), then the consumer is entitled to have the credit bureau investigate and correct the inaccuracy. As previously discussed, if the credit bureau is unable to correct the inaccuracy within a reasonable amount of time, the entire bankruptcy must be removed from the credit report. Many credit correction agencies will continue challenging different inaccuracies in the bankruptcy until it is finally removed or 100% correct. In some cases certain credit correction agencies will even deny that the bankruptcy belonged to their client in the first place.

The above applies the same to Judgment and Liens. In part 4 of this course, Bankruptcies (Chapter 7) and The Wage Earner Plan (Chapter 13) are further discussed in detail, including alternatives available to the consumer other than Bankruptcy.

Location of Major Credit Bureaus

As previously discussed, in the United States there are five major credit bureaus. Credit information on almost every adult resident of America is contained in the files of at least one of the bureaus. If you need to contact them, call or write requesting the address of their closest branch office.

TRW Credit Information Service
500 City Park West
Orange, CA 92667
(714) 991-5100

Trans Union Credit Information
444 No. Michigan Avenue
Chicago, IL 60611
(312) 645-6000

CBI/EQUIFAX
5505 Peachtree Dunwoody Rd.
Atlanta, GA 30302
(404) 250-4000 / (800) 685-1111

Associated Credit Services
2505 Fannin Street
Houston, Texas 77002
(713) 652-3360

Chilton Group/Creditmatic Systems
P. O. Box 2049
Dallas, Texas 75221
(214) 699-6111

> See the U. S. maps on the following pages for the bureaus that serve you.

Credit Bureau Coverage Map:
TRW Credit Information System Coverage

Nationwide Coverage

TRW Credit Information Services

500 City Park West
Orange, California 92667

(714) 991-5100

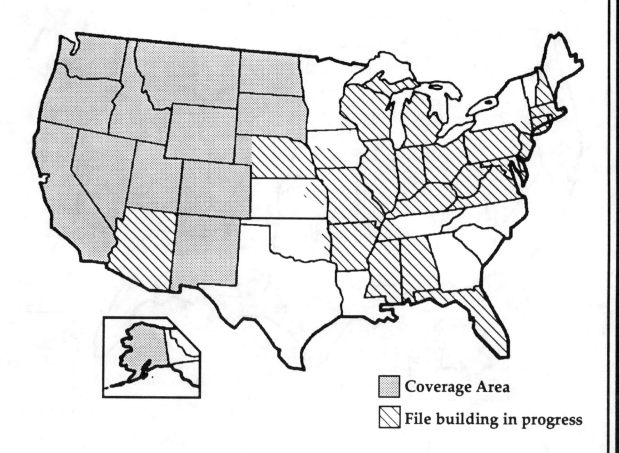

Coverage Area

File building in progress

Trans Union Credit Information

444 No. Michigan Avenue
Chicago, Illinois 60611

(312) 645-6000

Credit Bureau Coverage Map:
CBI/EQUIFAX Coverage

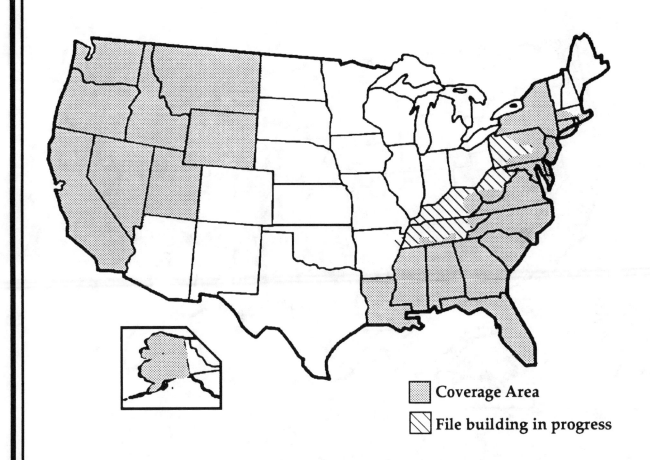

Coverage Area

File building in progress

CBI/EQUIFAX Company

5505 Peachtree Dunwoody Rd.
Atlanta, Georgia 30302

(404) 250-4000
1-(800) 685-1111

Credit Bureau Coverage Map:
Associated Credit Services Coverage

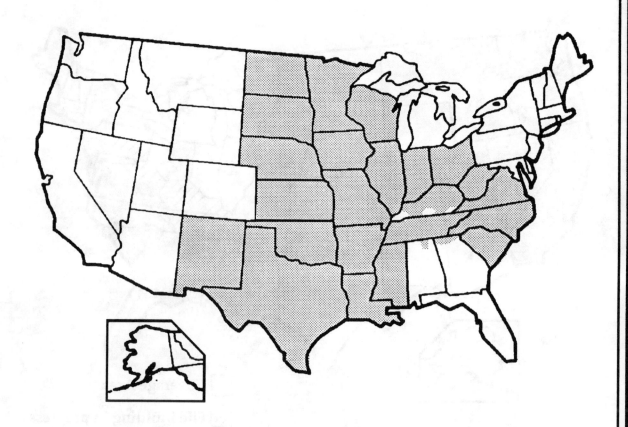

Associated Credit Services

2505 Fannin Street
Houston, Texas 77002

(713) 652-3360

Chilton Group/Creditmatic Systems Coverage

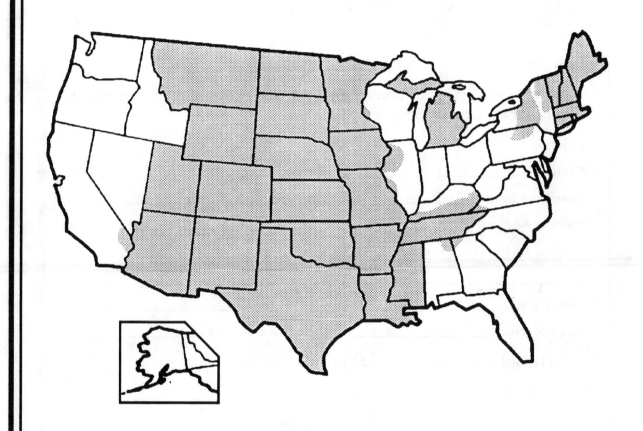

Chilton Group/Creditmatic Systems

P. O. Box 2049
Dallas, Texas 75221

(214) 699-6111

Date:_____

ATTN: Customer Relations Department

Dear Sir:

   At your earliest opportunity, please mail me a copy of my credit report. The information needed is listed below.

Name: _____ **Spouse:** _____

Present Address: _____

Previous Address: _____

Previous Address (Last 5 years): _____

_____

Date of Birth: _____

Soc. Sec. No.: _____ **Spouse Soc. Sec. No.:** _____

Credit Denied Last 30 Days?   ❏ **Yes**   ❏ **No**

Credit Denied By: _____

Check for $ _____ (each person) enclosed.

Thank you.

Yours truly,

Formal Complaints and the
Federal Trade Commission

If a consumer feels a credit bureau has violated his rights, he should immediately file a formal written complain with the Federal Trade Commission. It may be a good idea for the consumer to initiate his protest with a phone call to the F.T.C. Find below a list of F.T.C. regional offices, as well as their headquarters in Washington.

Headquarters:

Federal Trade Commission
Pennsylvania Avenue and 6th Street, N.W.
Washington, D.C. 20580
(202) 523-3830

Regional Offices:

1718 Peachtree Street, N.W., Atlanta, Georgia 30367, (404) 347-4836.

150 Causeway Street, Boston, Massachusetts 02114, (617) 223-6621

55 East Monroe Street, Chicago, Illinois 60603, (312) 353-4423

118 St. Clair Avenue, Cleveland, Ohio 44114, (216) 522-4207

8303 Elmbrook Drive, Dallas, Texas 75247, (214) 767-7050

1405 Curtis Street, Denver, Colorado 80201 (303) 837-2271

11000 Wilshire Boulevard, Los Angeles, California 90024, (213) 209-7575

25 Federal Plaza, New York, New York 10278, (212) 264-1207

450 Golden Gate Avenue, San Francisco, California 94102, (415) 556-1270

915 Second Avenue, Seattle, Washington 98174, (206) 442-4655

Adding Favorable Items To Credit Reports

As previously explained, not all of a consumer's credit appears in his credit report. The consumer may have some good credit he may want to appear. The Fair Credit Reporting Act does not specifically make reference to this; however, the Federal Trade Commission has advised credit bureaus that if a consumer credit report is derogatory in content and results in credit denial, the consumer should be able to supplement his report in order for it to be more demonstrative of his overall payment history. Many credit bureaus will provide this service for a small fee.

Once the consumer has completed correcting his credit report, at his option he can have the credit bureau send the latest copy of his report to anyone who has run a report on him for the past six (6) months (employers – 2 years). It is a good idea for the consumer to get a current copy of his credit report every few months, even if he is not presently applying for credit. He should do this in order to make sure his report is accurate at all times. Remember, **the consumer's goal is to control what is reported on his credit report at all times.**

Multiple Credit Reports

This section is an educational analysis which deals with multiple/alternate credit reports, a moderately common occurrence where a consumer has two credit reports. This phenomenon is the result of the tremendous volume of information contained in the credit bureau's computers and the computer's information retrieval system. In recent times several west coast attorneys have been using this flaw in the credit reporting system by setting up alternate credit reports for their clients. They justify this practice by pointing out certain credit bureaus blatant disregard for consumers' rights.

We have heard of fees ranging from $750 to $3,000 for setting up alternate credit reports.

Alternate credit reports happen much more often by accident than by design.

The attorneys that we have spoken to involved in this practice feel that having an alternate credit file **does not** necessarily mean any law has been broken (especially since it happens so often by accident); provided the alternate report is not used for fraud or deceit.

What Is An Alternate File?

An alternate credit report is exactly what the name implies; a consumer having two (2) credit reports (usually one good, and one bad if purposely set up) and each credit report being autonomous or separate of each other. Depending on how the applicant applies for credit is how one of the reports is found (pulled). Usually alternate credit reports are purposely created when a client's credit report is beyond repair. People involved in this practice feel it is a last resource which is **extremely effective.** Contrary to popular belief, setting up an alternate report does **not** involve a new social security number or identity. In my process of gathering information for this manual and helping people correct their credit, I have come across people for whom the computer has accidentally created new reports without their even knowing it. They did not understand why their credit was good on some occasions and bad on others. This illustrates how simple and effective alternate reports can be.

How Do Alternate Files Occur?

To analyze how an alternate report can occur we must first look at how a consumer's credit report is found among the millions of other credit reports.

All major credit bureaus use computers to access credit reports. A computer is merely a machine that does exactly what it is told to do. It records information it is told to, it deletes information it is told to, and prints a credit report on someone when told to do so (assuming it is given the right information). It is estimated that the largest credit bureau in America has in excess of 200 million credit reports on file. If there are only 150 million adults in America over the age of 18, where did the other 50 million plus reports come from? So, how does the computer find a consumer among the other 200 million potential reports? Obviously, the computer has to be given a command with specific information on the consumer in order to find the consumer's file. Each bureau has their own method of programming their computers for data retrieval. In the hypothetical example used below, the computer is programmed to pick up the first two (2) symbols of each item of information form a code which quickly accesses the consumer's file.

For Example:

Name:	DOE, JOHN M.
Address:	121,ELM,ST,CORAL GABLES,FL
Social Security:	999-16-3614

The computer reads: DOJOMO12ELSTCOGAFL99 and looks for a file with this heading. If the computer cannot find a file with this heading, or moderately close to match with the initialized information, it reports "NO FILE ON RECORD" or something to that effect. The computer can only access something very close to this heading, if not, it may find several hundred or thousand files.

Let's assume John M. Doe's address on Elm Street was only a temporary address while attending college and he moves back to his parents house, his permanent address, in Peoria, Illinois.

For Example:

Name:	DOE, JOHN M.
Address:	211,MAIN,ST,PEORIA,IL
Social Security:	999-16-3614

The computer would read: DOJOMO21MASTPEIL99

as opposed to: DOJOMO12ELSTCOFL99

If John fills in a credit application without listing his Coral Gables address (previous address) there is very little chance of picking up his credit report from Florida (regardless if the report is good, bad or indifferent). Some credit bureaus, even if he had listed his previous address, may not have any information on the State of Florida and it would still read only the information on John prior to his going away to college. The same would have applied to John when he moved to Florida for the first time.

Even though this example is separated by hundreds of miles, alternate files can occur in the consumer's city, with the same credit bureau; in many cases while the consumer is still living in the same house! The most important variable for the computer in accessing a person's file is their address and zip code as one unit and the name and social security number as one unit (unless you have an extremely unusual last name and live in a very small town). People who have moved on a couple of occasions in the last couple of years appear to be prime candidates for alternate credit files.

The actual mechanics of an alternate file are quite simple. The people we spoke to for whom the computers accidentally had created a new file had basically the following in common: First, they filled in a credit application (or requested a copy of their credit history from the credit bureau) truthfully, however, omitting certain information (this information will vary from bureau to bureau, depending on their computer data retrieval method). If done intentionally, we have heard of individuals who write down three or four sets of factual information on themselves and then go out to three or four different car dealers submitting one of the different sets of information until one comes back and says "NO RECORD". For example, if you moved three times in the last three years and the credit application only has room for one previous address, or a woman who just married and the application does not request her maiden name.

Once a combination of truthfulness on an application results in a "NO RECORD FOUND", or an empty file, the applicant must start creating a credit history from scratch as if they never had credit before.

The drawback of alternate credit files is the time it takes to create; 1 to 18 months. However, many people involved in the practice feel it is better than waiting the several years it takes to repair a non-repairable credit report. **The individual has to be very careful to always fill in information on a credit application the same way that it is on his new report so both reports won't cross reference each other.**

Essentially, what an alternate file does is bury the old report in the millions upon millions of other reports, only to be retrieved when the time limitations require all derogatory information be removed from the old report.

Merging / Piggy-Back

Another variation of an alternate report theme, which is especially effective for women with bad credit, is when they marry and **piggy-back**, or merge onto their new husband's credit report (assuming he has good credit). This is facilitated by the fact that they have a new name and address. This can be easily accomplished by using a variation of the techniques previously explained in the alternate file section.

SAMPLE: Dispute Letter – Items appear in credit report which do not belong to the consumer.

Consumer's Name
Address
Social Security No.
Date of Birth
City/State/Zip

Date

Name of Credit Bureau
Street Address of Credit Bureau
City/State/Zip

ATTN: Customer Relations Department

Dear Sirs:

I am requesting that the following items listed below be immediately investigated. These items are <u>not</u> my account's or inquiries, *(if they belong to a former spouse, include that information)* and I would like them removed to reflect my true and accurate credit history. These inaccuracies are most injurious to my credit history.

Subscriber Name   *Subscriber #*   *Account #*

Additionally, the following credit inquiries were <u>not</u> authorized by me; I would like them removed.

Subscriber Name   *Subscriber #*   *Account #*

Please forward to me my updated credit report after you have completed your credit investigation.

Your cooperation in this matter is greatly appreciated.

Yours truly,
(Signature)
Name

SAMPLE: Dispute Letter – Items appear in credit report which are being inaccurately reported.

Consumer's Name
Address
Social Security No.
Date of Birth
City/State/Zip

Date

Name of Credit Bureau
Street Address of Credit Bureau
City/State/Zip

ATTN: Customer Relations Department

Dear Sirs:

I am requesting that the following items listed below be immediately investigated. These accounts have been paid promptly and satisfactorily and do not reflect my true and accurate credit history. These inaccuracies are most injurious and unfair to my credit history.

Subscriber Name   *Subscriber #*   *Account #*

Additionally, the following credit inquiries were not authorized by me; I would like them removed.

Subscriber Name   *Subscriber #*   *Account #*

Please forward to me my updated credit report after you have completed your credit investigation.

Your cooperation in this matter is greatly appreciated.

Yours truly,
(Signature)
Name

Consumer's Name
Address
Social Security No.
Date of Birth
City/State/Zip

Date

Name of Credit Bureau
Street Address of Credit Bureau
City/State/Zip

ATTN: Customer Relations Department

Dear Sirs:

I am in disagreement with the following items listed below which still appear on my credit report, even after your investigation. These incorrect items are highly injurious to my credit rating and are not true.

Subscriber Name	*Subscriber #*	*Account #*	*Reason Why Incorrect*

I would like the above list immediately re-investigated. Furthermore, in accordance with "The Fair Credit Reporting Act", Public Law 91-508 Title VI, Section 611, Subsections A-D, I would like the names and business addresses of each individual(s) with whom you verified the above, so that I may follow up.

Please forward to me my updated credit report after you have completed your credit investigation.

Your cooperation in this matter is greatly appreciated.

Yours truly,
(Signature)
Name

Consumer's Name
Address
Social Security No.
Date of Birth
City/State/Zip

Date

Name of Credit Bureau
Street Address of Credit Bureau
City/State/Zip

ATTN: Customer Relations Department

Dear Sirs:

Pursuant to the Fair Credit Reporting Act, Public Law 91-508, Title VI, Section 611 Sub Section B, I would like the following consumer statement added to my credit report.

"On *date*, I moved to my present address. At that time, I notified all of my creditors, including *name of creditor* of my new address. *Name of creditor* was very slow in changing my address on the monthly invoices to the correct one. As a result, several invoices were not received by me (and were not forwarded by the Post Office). The credit department at *name of creditor* made no effort to locate me, even though invoices were being returned to them. I notified *name of creditor* that I was not receiving their statements – it took them four weeks to figure out why! Upon receipt of all back-dated invoices, they were immediately paid in full. Unbeknownst to me, *name of creditor* was reporting my account as being late at the credit bureau. I first became aware of this when I went to apply for a car loan.

I have repeatedly asked the credit department at *name of creditor* to please clarify this misleading information on my credit report. Unfortunately, they have pursued this request with the same amount of efficiency, energy and zeal as they used to forward my mail to my correct address in the first place."

Please send me a copy of my updated credit report once the above has been completed. The above statement is most important to the unjust manner in which the above is presently being reflected on my credit report.

Your cooperation in this matter is greatly appreciated.

Yours truly,
(Signature)
Name

Consumer's Name
Address
Social Security No.
Date of Birth
City/State/Zip

Date

Name of Credit Bureau
Street Address of Credit Bureau
City/State/Zip

ATTN: Customer Relations Department

Dear Sirs:

At your earliest opportunity I would like you to please list the following credit references on my credit report:

Subscriber Name   *Subscriber #*   *Account #*

Please send me an updated credit report once the above has been completed. If there is any expense for this service, please advise.

Your cooperation in this matter is greatly appreciated.

Yours truly,
(Signature)
Name

Consumer's Name
Address
Social Security No.
Date of Birth
City/State/Zip

Date

Name of Credit Bureau
Street Address of Credit Bureau
City/State/Zip

ATTN: Customer Relations Department

Dear Sirs:

On *date letter was sent,* I sent you a letter requesting several items be investigated on my credit report. (Please see enclosed copy.)

As of yet I have not received a response from you. Under the Fair Credit Reporting Act you are required to respond within a "reasonable" period of time. Please be advised that unless my credit investigation is not completed I will file a formal complaint with the Federal Trade Commission. I hope this will not be necessary.

Yours truly,
(Signature)
Name

Enclosure

SAMPLE: Request Letter – Inquiring as to identity of persons or businesses pulling unauthorized credit reports.

Consumer's Name
Address
Social Security No.
Date of Birth
City/State/Zip

Date

Name of Credit Bureau
Street Address of Credit Bureau
City/State/Zip

ATTN: Decoding Department

Dear Sirs:

At your first opportunity please provide me with the names, addresses, and phone numbers of the following subscribers:

Subscriber Name   _Subscriber #_   _Date of Report_

These subscribers have run unauthorized credit reports on me (please see enclosed credit report) and I wish to contact them to inquire why.

Your cooperation in this matter is greatly appreciated.

Yours truly,
(_Signature_)
Name

Enclosure

Consumer's Name
Address
Social Security No.
Date of Birth
City/State/Zip

Date

Name of Creditor/Dealership who ran illegal report
Name of President or General Manager
Street Address
City/State/Zip

Dear Mr./Ms. _____:

It has come to my attention that your company, on *date of inquiry* illegally ran a credit report on me. At no time did I ever authorize you to do this. This action on your part constitutes a violation of my rights under the Fair Credit Reporting Act, and is highly injurious to my credit rating. (I have enclosed a copy of this Act for your review.)

Unless you immediately contact the credit bureau and remedy this situation, I will have no choice but to take legal action.

Please govern yourself accordingly.

Yours truly,
(Signature)
Name

Enclosure

cc: Name of Credit Bureau

Free Publications from the Governors of the Federal Reserve

The following **free publications** are available from the Board of Governors of the Federal Reservice System. It is highly recommended for you to acquire and keep them for future reference.

Consumer Handbook to Credit Protection Laws – Explains consumer credit laws, helps in acquiring a good credit profile.

The Equal Credit Opportunity Act and Age – Describes lending criteria used in ascertaining credit-worthiness; also deals with the topic of age discrimination as pertaining to credit procurement.

Equal Credit Opportunity Act and Women – Explains the effects of Equal Credit Opportunity Act as it applies to women.

Fair Credit Billing – Deals with billing errors on open-end credit accounts.

How To File A Consumer Credit Complaint – Explains how to file a formal complaint against a bank in connection with federal credit laws.

If You Use A Credit Card – Explains the protection under federal laws against lost cards, what to do if goods bought with credit cards are unsatisfactory.

What Truth In Leasing Means To You – Explains major provisions of the Truth in Leasing Act.

Publications can be obtained by writing:

Board of Governors of the Federal Reserve System, Publication Services
20th and C Streets N.W., Washington DC 20551, (202)452-3000

The Federal Reserve can provide the consumer with an abundance of current financial information. They publish weekly letters, economic reviews and annual reports. For information, contact the Federal Reserve at one of these addresses:

Federal Reserve Bank of Chicago, Public Information Department,
230 South LaSalle Street, Chicago, IL 60590, (312) 322-5322

Federal Reserve Bank of St. Louis, Bank Relations & Public Information Department,
411 Locust Street, St. Louis, MO 63102, (314) 444-8444

Federal Reserve Bank of Minneapolis, Public Information Department,
250 Marquette Avenue, Minneapolis, MN 55480, (816) 340-2345

Federal Reserve Bank of Kansas City, Public Information Department,
925 Grand Avenue, Kansas City, MO 64198, (816) 881-2000

Federal Reserve Addresses, continued:

Federal Reserve Bank of Dallas, Public Information Department,
400 South Akard Street, Dallas, TX 75222, (214) 651-6111

Federal Reserve Bank of San Francisco, Public Information Department,
101 Market Street, San Francisco, CA 94105, (415) 974-2000

Federal Reserve Bank of Boston, Public Information Department,
600 Atlantic Avenue, Boston, MA 02106, (617) 973-3000

Federal Reserve Bank of New York, Public Information Department,
33 Liberty Street, New York NY 10045, (212) 720-5000

Federal Reserve Bank of Philadelphia, Public Information Department,
Ten Independence Mall, Philadelphia, PA 19106, (215) 574-6000

Federal Reserve Bank of Cleveland, Research Department,
1455 East Sixth Street, Cleveland, OH 44101, (216) 579-2000

Federal Reserve Bank of Richmond, Bank & Public Relations Department,
701 East Byrd Street, Richmond, VA 23261, (804) 697-8000

Federal Reserve Bank of Atlanta, Research Department, Publications Unit,
104 Marietta Street, N.W., Atlanta, GA 30303, (404) 521-8500

TITLE VI – PROVISIONS RELATING TO CREDIT REPORTING AGENCIES
Amendment of Consumer Protection Act

Sec. 601. The Consumer Credit Protection Act is amended by adding at the end thereof the following new title:

"Title VI - CONSUMER CREDIT REPORTING"

"Sec.
"601. Short title.
"602. Findings and purpose.
"603. Definitions and rules of construction.
"604. Permissible purposes of reports.
"605. Obsolete information.
"606. Disclosure of investigative consumer reports.
"607. Compliance procedures.
"608. Disclosures to governmental agencies.
"609. Disclosure to consumers.
"610. Conditions of disclosure to consumers.
"611. Procedure in case of disputed accuracy.
"612. Charges for certain disclosures.
"613. Public record information for employment purposes.
"614. Restrictions on investigative consumer reports.
"615. Requirements on users of consumer reports.
"616. Civil liability for willful noncompliance.
"617. Civil liability for negligent noncompliance.
"618. Jurisdiction of courts: limitation of actions.
"619. Obtaining information under false pretenses.
"620. Unauthorized disclosures by officers or employees.
"621. Administrative enforcement.
"622. Relation to State laws.

"§601 Short Title

"This title may be cited as the Fair Credit Reporting Act.

"§601. Findings and purpose

"(a) The Congress makes the following findings:

"(1) The banking system is dependent upon fair and accurate credit reporting. Inaccurate credit reports directly impair the efficiency of the banking system, and unfair credit reporting methods undermine the public confidence which is essential to the continued functioning of the banking system.

"(2) An elaborate mechanism has been developed for investigating and evaluating the credit worthiness, credit standing, credit capacity, character and general reputation of consumers.

"(3) Consumer reporting agencies have assumed a vital role in assembling and evaluating consumer credit and other information on consumers.

"(4) There is a need to insure that consumer reporting agencies exercise their grave responsibilities with fairness, impartiality, and a respect for the consumer's right to privacy.

"(b) It is the purpose of this title to require that consumer reporting agencies adopt reasonable procedures for meeting the needs of commerce for consumer credit, personnel, insurance, and other information in a manner which is fair and equitable to the consumer, with regard to the confidentiality, accuracy, relevancy, and proper utilization of such information in accordance with the requirements of this title.

"§602. *Definitions and rules of construction*

"(a) Definitions and rules of construction set forth in this section are applicable for the purposes of this title.

"(b) The term 'person' means any individual, partnership, corporation, trust, estate, cooperative, association, government or governmental subdivision or agency, or other entity.

"(c) The term 'consumer' means an individual.

"(d) The term 'consumer report' means any written, oral, or other communication of any information by a consumer reporting agency bearing on a consumer's credit worthiness, credit standing, credit capacity, character, general reputation, personal characteristics, or mode of living which is used or expected to be used or collected in whole or in part for the purpose of serving as a factor in establishing the consumer's eligibility for (1) credit or insurance to be used primarily for personal, family, or household purposes, or (2) employment purposes, or (3) other purposes authorized under section 604. The term does not include (A) any report containing information solely as to transactions or experiences between the consumer and the person making the report; (B) any authorization or approval of a specific extension of credit directly or indirectly by the issuer of a credit card or similar device; or (C) any report in which a person who has been requested by a third party to make a specific extension of credit directly or indirectly to a consumer conveys his decision with respect to such request, if the third party advises the consumer of the name and address of the person to whom the request was made and such person makes the disclosures to the consumer required under section 615.

"(e) The term 'investigative consumer report' means a consumer report or portion thereof in which information on a consumer's character, general reputation, personal characteristics, or mode of living is obtained through personal interviews with neighbors, friends, or associates of the consumer reported on or with others with whom he is acquainted or who may have knowledge concerning any such items of information. However, such information shall not include specific factual information on a consumer's credit record obtained directly from a creditor of the consumer or from a consumer reporting agency when such information was obtained directly from a creditor of the consumer or from the consumer.

"(f) The term 'consumer reporting agency' means any person which, for monetary fees, dues, or on a cooperative non-profit basis, regularly engages in whole or in part in the practice

REFERENCE: The Fair Credit Reporting Act, continued

of assembling or evaluating consumer credit information or other information on consumers for the purpose of furnishing consumer reports to third parties, and which uses any means or facility of interstate commerce for the purpose of preparing or furnishing consumer reports.

"(g) The term 'file', when used in connection with information on any consumer, means all of the information on that consumer recorded and retained by a consumer reporting agency regardless of how the information is stored.

"(h) The term 'employment purposes' when used in connection with a consumer report means a report used for the purpose of evaluating a consumer for employment, promotion, reassignment or retention as an employee.

"(i) The term 'medical information' means information or records obtained, with the consent of the individual to whom it relates, from licensed physicians or medical practitioners, hospitals, clinics, or other medical or medically related facilities.

"§604. Permissible purposes of reports

"A consumer reporting agency may furnish a consumer report under the following circumstances and no other:

"(1) In response to the order of a court having jurisdiction to issue such an order.

"(2) In accordance with the written instructions of the consumer to whom it relates.

"(3) To a person which it has reason to believe –

"(A) intends to use the information in connection with a credit transaction involving the consumer on whom the information is to be furnished an involving the extension of credit to, or review or collection of an account of, the consumer; or

"(B) intends to use the information for employment purposes; or

"(C) intends to use the information in connection with the underwriting of insurance involving the consumer; or

"(D) intends to use the information in connection with a determination of the consumer's eligibility for a license or other benefit granted by a governmental instrumentality required by law to consider an applicant's financial responsibility or status; or

"(E) otherwise has a legitimate business need for the information in connection with a business transaction involving the consumer.

"§605. Obsolete information

"(a) Except as authorized under subsection (b), no consumer reporting agency may make any consumer report containing any of the following items of information:

"(1) Cases under title 11 of the United States Code or under the Bankruptcy Act that, from the date of entry of the order for relief or the date of adjudication, as the cause may be, antedate the report by more than 10 years.

"(2) Suites and judgments which, from date of entry, antedate the report by more than

THE CREDIT IMPROVEMENT AND PROTECTION HANDBOOK 37

seven years or until the governing statute of limitations has expired, whichever is the longer period.

"(3) Paid tax liens which, from date of payment, antedate the report by more than seven years.

"(4) Accounts placed for collection or charged to profit and loss which antedate the report by more than seven years.

"(5) Records of arrest, indictment, or conviction of crime which, from date of disposition, release, or parole, antedate the report by more than seven years.

"(6) Any other adverse item of information which antedates the report by more than seven years.

"(b) The provisions of subsection (a) are not applicable in the case of any consumer credit report to used in connection with –

"(1) a credit transaction involving, or which may reasonably be expected to involve, a principal amount of $50,000 or more;

"(2) the underwriting of life insurance involving, or which may reasonably be expected to involve, a face amount of $50,000 or more; or

"(3) the employment of any individual at an annual salary which equals, or which may reasonably be expected to equal $20,000, or more.

"§606. Disclosure of investigative consumer reports

"(a) A person may not procure or cause to be prepared an investigative consumer report on any consumer unless –

"(1) it is clearly and accurately disclosed to the consumer that an investigative consumer report including information as to his character, general reputation, personal characteristics, and mode of living, whichever are applicable, may be made, and such disclosure is (A) made in a writing mailed, or otherwise delivered, to the consumer, not later than three days after the date on which the report was first requested, and (B) includes a statement informing the consumer of his right to request the additional disclosures provided under subsection (b) of this section; or

"(2) the report is to be used for employment purposes for which the consumer has not specifically applied.

"(b) Any person who procures or causes to be prepared an investigative consumer report on any consumer shall, upon written request made by the consumer within a reasonable period of time after the receipt by him of the disclosure required by subsection (a)(1), shall make a complete and accurate disclosure of the nature and scope of the investigation requested. This disclosure shall be made in a writing mailed, or otherwise delivered, to the consumer not later than five days after the date on which the request for such disclosure was received from the consumer or such report was first requested, whichever is the later.

"(c) No person may be held liable for any violation of subsection (a) or (b) of this section if he shows by a preponderance of the evidence that at the time of the violation he maintained reasonable procedures to assure compliance with subsection (a) or (b).

"§607. Compliance procedures

"(a) Every consumer reporting agency shall maintain reasonable procedures designed to avoid violations of section 605 and to limit the furnishing of consumer reports to the purposes listed under section 604. These procedures shall require that prospective users of the information identify themselves, certify the purposes for which the information is sought, and certify that the information will be used for no other purpose. Every consumer reporting agency shall make a reasonable effort to verify the identity of a new prospective user and the uses certified by such prospective user prior to furnishing such user a consumer report. No consumer reporting agency may furnish a consumer report to any person if it has reasonable grounds for believing that the consumer report will not be used for a purpose listed in section 604.

"(b) Whenever a consumer reporting agency prepares a consumer report it shall follow reasonable procedures to assure maximum possible accuracy of the information concerning the individual about whom the report relates.

"§608. Disclosures to governmental agencies

"Notwithstanding the provisions of section 604, a consumer reporting agency may furnish identifying information respecting any consumer, limited to his name, address, former addresses, places of employment, or former places of employment, to a governmental agency.

"§609. Disclosures to consumers

"(a) Every consumer reporting agency shall, upon request and proper identification of any consumer, clearly and accurately disclose to the consumer:

"(1) The nature and substance of all information (except medical information) in its files on the consumer at the time of the request.

"(2) The sources of the information; except that the sources of information acquired solely for use in preparing an investigative consumer report and actually used for no other purpose need not be disclosed: Provided, that in the event an action is brought under this title, such sources shall be available to the plaintiff under appropriate discovery procedures in the court in which the action is brought.

"(3) The recipients of any consumer report on the consumer which it has furnished –

"(A) for employment purposes within the two-year period preceding the request, and

"(B) for any other purpose within the six-month period preceding the request.

"(b) The requirements of subsection (a) respecting the disclosure of sources of information and the recipients of consumer reports do not apply to information received or consumer reports furnished prior to the effective date of this title except to the extent that the matter involved is contained in the files of the consumer reporting agency on that date.

"§610. Conditions of disclosure to consumers

"(a) A consumer reporting agency shall make the disclosures required under section 609 during normal business hours and on reasonable notice.

"(b) The disclosures required under section 609 shall be made to the consumer –

"(1) in person if he appears in person and furnishes proper identification; or

"(2) by telephone if he has made a written request, with proper identification, for telephone disclosure and the toll charge, if any, for the telephone call is prepaid by or charged directly to the consumer.

"(c) Any consumer reporting agency shall provide trained personnel to explain to the consumer any information furnished to him pursuant to section 609.

"(d) The consumer shall be permitted to be accompanied by one other person of his choosing, who shall furnish reasonable identification. A consumer reporting agency may require the consumer to furnish a written statement granting permission to the consumer reporting agency to discuss the consumer's file in such person's presence.

"(e) Except as provided in sections 616 and 617, no consumer may bring any action or proceeding in the nature of of defamation, invasion of privacy, or negligence with respect to the reporting of information against any consumer reporting agency, any user of information, or any person who furnishes information to a consumer reporting agency, based on information disclosed pursuant to section 609, 610 or 615, except as to false information furnished with malice or willful intent to injure such consumer.

"§611. Procedure in case of disputed accuracy

"(a) If the completeness or accuracy of any item of information contained in his file is disputed by a consumer, and such dispute is directly conveyed to the consumer reporting agency by the consumer, the consumer reporting agency shall within a reasonable period of time reinvestigate and record the current status of that information unless it has reasonable grounds to believe that the dispute by the consumer is frivolous or irrelevant. If after such reinvestigation such information is found to be inaccurate or can no longer be verified, the consumer reporting agency shall promptly delete such information. The presence of contradictory information in the consumer's file does not in and of itself constitute reasonable grounds for believing the dispute is frivolous or irrelevant.

"(b) If the reinvestigation does not resolve the dispute, the consumer may file a brief statement setting forth the nature of the dispute. The consumer reporting agency may limit such statements to not more than one hundred words if it provided the consumer with assistance in writing a clear summary of the dispute.

"(c) Whenever a statement of a dispute is filed, unless there is reasonable grounds to believe that it is frivolous or irrelevant, the consumer reporting agency shall, in any subsequent consumer report containing the information in question, clearly note that it is disputed by the consumer and provide either the consumer's statement or a clear and accurate codification or summary thereof.

"(d) Following any deletion of information which is found to be inaccurate or whose accuracy can no longer be verified or any notation as to disputed information, the consumer reporting agency shall, at the request of the consumer, furnish notification that the item has been deleted or the statement, codification or summary pursuant to subsection (b) or (c) to any person specifically designated by the consumer who has within two years prior thereto received a consumer report for employment purposes, or within six months prior thereto received a consumer report for any other purpose, which contained the deleted or disputed information. The consumer reporting agency shall clearly and conspicuously disclose to the consumer his rights to make such a request. Such disclosure shall be made at or prior to the time the information is deleted or the consumer's statement regarding the disputed information is received.

"§612. *Charges for certain disclosures.*

"A consumer reporting agency shall make all disclosures pursuant to section 609 and furnish all consumer report pursuant to section 611(d) without charge to the consumer if, within thirty days after receipt by such consumer of a notification pursuant to section 615 or notification from a debt collection agency affiliated with such consumer reporting agency stating that the consumer's credit rating my be or has been adversely affected, the consumer makes a request under section 609 or 611(d). Otherwise, the consumer reporting agency may impose a reasonable charge on the consumer for making disclosure to such consumer pursuant to section 609, the charge for which shall be indicated to the consumer prior to making disclosure; and for furnishing notifications, statements, summaries, or codifications to person designated by the consumer pursuant to section 611(d), the charge for which shall be indicated to the consumer prior to furnishing such information and shall not exceed the charge that the consumer reporting agency would impose on each designated recipient for a consumer report except that no charge may be made for notifying such persons of the deletion of information which is found to be inaccurate or which can no longer be verified.

"§613. *Public record information for employment purposes*

"A consumer reporting agency which furnishes a consumer report for employment purposes and which for that purpose compiles and reports items of information on consumers which are matters of public record and are likely to have adverse effect upon a consumer's ability to obtain employment shall –

"(1) at the time such public record information is reported to the user of such consumer report, notify the consumer of the fact that public record information is being reported by the consumer reporting agency, together with the name and address of the person to whom such information is being reported; or

"(2) maintain strict procedures designed to insure that whenever public record information which is likely to have an adverse effect on a consumer's ability to obtain employment is reported it is complete and up to date. For purposes of this paragraph, items of public record relating to arrests, indictments, convictions, suits, tax liens, and outstanding judgments shall be considered up to date if the current public record status of the item at the time of the report is reported.

"§614. Restrictions on investigative consumer reports

"Whenever a consumer reporting agency prepares an investigative consumer report, no adverse information in the consumer report (other than information which is a matter of public record) may be included in a subsequent consumer report unless such adverse information has been verified in the process of making such subsequent consumer report, or the adverse information was received within the three-month period preceding the date the subsequent report is furnished.

"§615. Requirements on users of consumer reports

"(a) Whenever credit or insurance for personal, family, or household purposes, or employment involving a consumer is denied or the charge for such credit or insurance is increased either wholly or partly because of information contained in a consumer report from a consumer reporting agency, the user of the consumer report shall so advise the consumer against whom such adverse action has been taken and supply the name and address of the consumer reporting agency making the report.

"(b) Whenever credit for personal, family, or household purposes involving a consumer is denied or the charge for such credit is increased either wholly or partly because of information obtained from a person other than a consumer reporting agency bearing upon the consumer's credit worthiness, credit standing, credit capacity, character, general reputation, personal characteristics, or mode of living, the user of such information shall, within a reasonable period of time, upon the consumer's written request for the reasons for such adverse action received within sixty days after learning of such adverse action, disclose the nature of the information to the the consumer. The use of such information shall clearly and accurately disclose to the consumer his right to make such written request at the time such adverse action is communicated to the consumer.

"(c) No person shall be held liable for any violation of this section if he shows a preponderance of the evidence that at the time of the alleged violation he maintained reasonable procedures to assure compliance with the provisions of subsections (a) and (b).

"§616. Civil liability for willful noncompliance

"Any consumer reporting agency or use of information which willfully fails to comply with any requirement imposed under this title with respect to any consumer is liable to that consumer in an amount equal to the sum of –

"(1) any actual damages sustained by the consumer as a result of the failure;

"(2) such amount of punitive damages as the court may allow; and

"(3) in the case of any successful action to enforce any liability under this section, the costs of the action together with reasonable attorney's fees as determined by the court.

"§617. Civil liability for negligent noncompliance

"Any consumer reporting agency or use of information which is negligent in failing to comply with any requirement imposed under this title with respect to any consumer is liable to that consumer in an amount equal to the some of –

"(1) any actual damages sustained by the consumer as a result of the failure;

"(2) in the case of any successful action to enforce any liability under this section, the costs of the action together with reasonable attorney's fees as determined by the court.

"§618. Jurisdiction of courts; limitation of actions

"An action to enforce any liability created under this title may be brought in any appropriate United States district court without regard to the amount in controversy, or in any other court of competent jurisdiction, within two years from the date on which the liability arises, except that where a defendant has materially and willfully misrepresented any information required under this title to be disclosed to an individual and the information so misrepresented is material to the establishment of the defendant's liability to that individual under this title, the action may be brought at any time within two years after discovery by the individual of the misrepresentations.

"§619. Obtaining information under false pretenses

"Any person who knowingly and willfully obtains information on a consumer from a consumer reporting agency under false pretenses shall be fined not more than $5,000 or imprisoned not more than one year, or both.

"§620. Unauthorized disclosures by officers and employees

"Any officer or employee of a consumer reporting agency who knowingly and willfully provides information concerning an individual from the agency's files to a person not authorized to receive that information shall be fined not more than $5,000 or imprisoned not more than one year, or both.

"§621. Administrative enforcement

"(a) Compliance with the requirement imposed under this title shall be enforced under the Federal Trade Commission Act by the Federal Trade Commission with respect to consumer reporting agencies and all other persons subject thereto, except to the extent that enforcement of the requirements imposed under this title is specifically committed to some other government agency under subsection (b) hereof. For the purpose of the exercise by the federal Trade Commission of its functions and powers under the Federal Trade Commission Act, a violation of any requirement or prohibition imposed under this title shall constitute an unfair or deceptive act or practice in commerce in violation of section 5(a) of the Federal Trade Commission Act and shall be subject to enforcement by the Federal Trade Commission under section 5(b) thereof with respect to any consumer reporting agency or person subject to enforcement powers by the Federal Trade Commission pursuant to this subsection, irrespective of whether that person is engaged in commerce or meets any other jurisdictional tests in the Federal Trade Commission Act. The Federal Trade Commission shall have such procedural, investigative, and enforcement powers, including the power to issue procedural rules in enforcing compliance with the requirement imposed under this title and to require the filing of reports, the production of documents, and the appearance of witnesses as though the applicable terms and conditions of the Federal Trade Commission Act were part of this title. Any person violating any of the provisions of this title shall be subject to the penalties and entitled to the privileges and immunities provided in the Federal Trade Commission Act as though the applicable terms and provisions thereof were part of this title.

"(b) Compliance with the requirements imposed under this title with respect to consumer reporting agencies and persons who use consumer reports from such agencies shall be enforced under –

"(1) section 8 of the Federal Deposit Insurance Ace, in the case of:

"(A) national banks, by the Comptroller of the Currency;

"(B) member banks of the Federal Reserve System (other than national banks), by the Federal Reserve Board; and

"(C) banks insured by the Federal Deposit Insurance Corporation (other than members of the Federal Reserve System), by the Board of Directors of the Federal Deposit Insurance Corporation.

"(2) section 5(d) of the Home Owners Loan Act of 1933, section 407 of the National Housing Act, and sections 6(i) and 17 of the Federal Home Loan Bank Act, by the Federal Home Loan Bank Board (acting directly or through the Federal Savings and Loan Insurance Corporation), in the case of any institution subject to any of those provisions;

"(3) the Federal Credit Union Act, by the Administrator of the National Credit Union Administration with respect to any Federal Credit Union;

"(4) the Acts to regulate commerce, by the Interstate Commerce Commission with respect to any common carrier subject to those Acts;

"(5) the Federal Aviation Act of 1958, by the Civil Aeronautics Board with respect to any air carrier or foreign air carrier subject to that Act; and

"(6) the Packers and Stockyards Act, 1921 (except as provided in section 406 of that Act), by the Secretary of Agriculture with respect to any activities subject that Act.

"(c) For the purpose of the exercise by any agency referred to in subsection (b) of its powers under any Act referred to in that subsection, a violation of any requirement imposed under this title shall be deemed to be a violation of a requirement imposed under that Act. In addition to its powers under any provision of law specifically referred to in subsection (b), each of the agencies referred to in that subsection may exercise, for the purpose of enforcing compliance with any requirement imposed under this title any other authority conferred on it by law.

"§622. *Relation to State laws*

"This title does not annul, alter, affect, or exempt any person subject to the provisions of this title from complying with the laws of any State with respect to the collection, distribution, or use of any information on consumers, except to the extent that those laws are inconsistent with any provision of this title, and then only to the extent of the inconsistency."

EFFECTIVE DATE

Sec. 602. Section 504 of the Consumer Credit Protection Act is amended by adding at the end thereof the following new subsection:

"(d) Title VI takes effect upon the expiration of one hundred and eighty days following the date of its enactment."

And the Senate agrees to the same.

PART TWO:
CREDIT CARDS
AND SETTLEMENT
COSTS

PART TWO: CREDIT CARDS AND SETTLEMENT COSTS

Credit Cards – A General Overview

Credit Cards have got to be considered one of the most incredible financial instruments of any era. Bank credit cards especially have experienced phenomenal growth in three short decades. Credit cards are nothing more than a plastic identification permitting consumers to buy almost anything. Credit cards have been incredibly effective as a marketing tool; they help produce sales. Because of high interest rates, **credit cards should be used exclusively as a convenience;** all balances should be paid off before finance charges are assessed (the interest rate banks charge on credit cards is 3 to 4 times greater than what they pay on savings accounts).

Despite recent lower interest rates on other types of loans, the rates charged on credit cards has remained high. Presently, the national average for bank credit cards is in excess of 18%. It is estimated that rates will continue at that level. There are three factors mainly responsible for this:

1. The losses suffered by banks (unsecured lending is one of the riskiest forms of lending).

2. About one-third of all cardholders pay them in full when due, therefore banks only charge interest on two-thirds of all purchases. Cardholders who maintain balances help defray the cost of cardholders who pay in full at the end of the month.

3. Your typical cardholder who makes minimum payments are not so much rate conscious, since monthly payment amounts are nominal.

Tax Reform Act and Credit Card Interest Expense

Under the Tax Reform Act of 1986, the interest rate expense incurred on credit cards as well as other consumer loans is no longer deductible from your federal income tax. As a result, a few banks are beginning to lower these rates in order to compensate for anticipated decline in credit card balances which are extended over a 30 day period. In general, however, as previously explained, it is expected for banks to maintain their interest rates on credit cards at peak levels.

The result of all this is that some banks are already charging 6% - 7% less than other banks. The best deal of all is to be able to pay your credit card balance in full at the end of the month (just use the card for convenience) and then the interest rate is irrelevant because it will always be zero (assuming you pay within the grace period). See "Banks with Low Credit Card Rates" later in this section.

Fraudulent Credit Card Billings
and What to Do

You may already have been contacted by one of the many telephone "boiler room" operations around the country. If so, you may have been told that you were selected to receive, or be awarded (but never that you have **won**) a new car, a free vacation, a VCR...

All you have to do to get the prize is supply the caller with your credit card number – either to verify identity, or for a guarantee that you will pay the sales tax, or some other excuse. Then, during the conversation, something is said, casually, about supplying a service or product.

Next thing you know, there's an unexplained $199 – $400 charge on your credit card! VISA says that their cardholders are losing as much as $50 million per year in such fraudulent billings.

What To Do!

1) **NEVER** give your credit card number to a person who calls you. Ordering by phone when *you* have called in response to an ethical ad is usually okay.

2) If stung, use your right to refuse to pay for the item and ask the card issuer to charge the amount back to the biller's account.

3) Always compare your receipts to your monthly card statement.

4) Be sure, when using your card, that the clerk returns you card and not someone else's; the cards are very similar and accidents do happen. An accidental switch is extremely inconvenient, especially if you are on a trip.

5) Always tear up the carbons in credit card slips, and always keep your copy of the bill. Credit card fraud is a common occurrence.

6) If your credit card is lost or stolen (or used without authorization), your liability is limited to only $50. Immediately report it stolen to the issuer. If there are any purchases made after your report, you will not be held liable for them. Even though your liability is limited to only $50 per card, most consumers carry 5 or 6 cards ($250 - $300). A solution may be a credit card protection service. For a modest fee, they will report all your cards stolen, get replacements, and insure you against your $50 liability.

Under the Fair Credit Billing Act, the consumer is able to withhold payment on a credit card purchase for merchandise or services provided which the consumer deemed substandard. The following four conditions must be met:

1. The charge must be in excess of $50.

2. The cardholder must attempt to settle the dispute directly with the merchant.

3. The cardholder must make the issuing institution aware of the dispute in writing (send via certified mail).

4. Merchant must be located with 100 miles of the cardholder's residence.

If there is a billing error on your monthly statement (charge for item(s) never purchased or you did not receive credit for a payment), you must notify the issuing card company in writing (formal letter) within sixty (60) days after the monthly statement was mailed to you (send via certified mail). They, in turn, must acknowledge the dispute within thirty (30) days.

At this point, the issuing company can either agree with you and make the appropriate changes by notifying you in writing, or send you a written explanation of why you are wrong and they are right. The issuing credit card company must be able to document any claims they make. During this dispute, the credit card company cannot refer the disputed amount for collection, report you as delinquent to the credit bureau, or revoke you card. This entire process cannot take longer than two billing cycles (not more than 90 days in total).

It is a good idea to always follow up any correspondence with a phone call. Always get the name of the person to whom you spoke and make notes. **Do not** record telephone calls, unless you immediately advise them of it before you start the conversation. If you do not advise them, you may be committing a crime.

If a cardholder requests an additional card for his spouse, the cardholder is responsible for full payment. If, in the future, he chooses to rescind the card's use by the spouse, he must immediately notify the issuing card company and simultaneously demand the card from the spouse. The cardholder will be responsible for all purchases until this is done.

Types of Credit Cards

Bank Cards – Mainly MasterCard® and Visa®

Offered primarily by banks, savings and loans, and some credit unions. MasterCard® (MasterCharge®, as originally known), was the "brainchild" of four prominent west coast banks who were looking to expand their consumer credit lending. What these banks did was offer local merchants the opportunity to in turn offer their clients the availability of credit. Basically, member banks agreed to accept the sales receipts of all member merchants. Banks were paid a nominal agreed upon percentage of the dollar sale. The advantages to the merchants are:

1. No accounts receivable. This eliminated credit risk and reduced their working capital requirements.

2. Banks were responsible for all collections, billing and bookkeeping.

Presently, most lending institutions establish their own credit criteria (billing policies, interest rates, annual fees, credit limits, etc., etc.). MasterCard® and Visa®

per sé do not issue the cards themselves. What they do is provide a clearing house. In fact, the bank name that appears on the card is not necessarily the issuing bank; it may be acting as a sales agent/representative for a major issuing bank. Consumer complaints regarding billing errors or something similar may have to be referred to the issuing bank, which may be out of state and not as cooperative as the bank from which they were originally obtained.

Presently, there are three states where the maximum interest rate is 5 percentage points over the federal discount rate, with a maximum (ceiling) of 17% per annum. They are Delaware, Oregon and Arkansas. However, **all banks in low interest states do not necessarily have low interest rates!** Many large federally chartered banks have relocated their credit card facilities to states that are more permissive on rates, and are able to issue these cards from other states.

Travel and Entertainment Cards – Most well known as American Express,® Diner's Club®and Carte Blanche®.

American Express® is accepted by almost twice as many business establishments as each of the other two. Travel and Entertainment cards have annual fees (around $50 per year); however, they require payment in full each month (no finance privilege). Travel and Entertainment cards have based their success on a marketing campaign emphasizing prestige and a host of unique services, such as free travel insurance, free traveler's cheques, emergency cash, check cashing, and no prepayment spending. Travel and Entertainment cards are geared toward the "executive/professional type", even though anyone may apply.

Travel and Entertainment cards are mainly accepted at hotels, restaurants, high-priced stores, and travel-oriented businesses. Recently, MasterCard® and Visa® have chosen to introduce their own Travel and Entertainment card by increasing the card's credit limit from the traditional $500 - $2,000 to $5,000 - $20,000. These cards are most commonly called Visa Gold® and Gold MasterCard®.

As might be expected, credit requirements on Travel and Entertainment cards are more stringent and accordingly, are more difficult to get.

Seller Credit Cards – Individual business charge account cards

This is the oldest, most widely known form of credit card. Issued and accepted exclusively by the issuing business establishment or chain (department stores, oil companies, airlines, car rental agencies, etc.). Originally conceived by the issuer in order to boost sales. Seldom is there an annual fee; billings and payback are almost identical to bank credit cards. Even though Seller Credit Cards' original purpose was to increase sales, because of the high interest rates that can be charged, many issuers are looking towards them as a profit center.

Debit Cards – Purchase amount is immediately deducted from cardholder's account

This is similar to a credit card, except all amounts charged on the card are immediately deducted from the cardholder's checking or savings account. If there are insufficient funds in the account, a debit cannot be made to it. Debits are immediately made possible by the use of "point of sale" equipment (P.O.S.). The most obvious disadvantage of Debit Cards is the lack of "float". To compensate for this, some banks are offering cash rebates on purchases made with the card. Banks are attracted to Debit Cards because they require a lot less processing time, work and expense than checks. The current trend is for major oil companies and, in the future, department stores to offer Debit Cards that can be used at their business locations.

Compared to other credit cards with "float", there are no advantages to the consumer for making payment with Debit Cards; other than convenience and knowing he cannot spend more than he has in his bank account. There has been one company that I am aware of that has given the consumer an incentive to use their own Debit Card, and I am quite sure others will follow soon. Kinko's, a chain of quick copy stores, uses this concept well. For every ten dollars you purchase on the card, you get eleven dollars worth of product or service.

One other disadvantage to the consumer is that this debit card cannot be used at any establishment other than the issuing business.

Banks Aggressively Looking to Issue Credit Cards

Banks which are aggressively seeking to issue credit cards may be more lenient on their credit requirements; they will tend to view the applicant more optimistically. In many cases, the applicant may be given the benefit of the doubt on marginal issues. There are several factors which banks take into consideration before an aggressive credit card issuing policy is enacted. These factors deal mainly in corporate policy, funds availability, market and economic constraints. Banks which are anxious to issue credit cards are banks with whom you want to do business.

However, banks which are aggressive today may not be in the near future. There are many factors which would cause a bank to become "unaggressive" in issuing credit cards. The five most common are:

1. They have achieved their quota.

2. Bad credit experiences and as a result, the institution becomes very stringent in their issue policy.

3. Changes in economic trends.

4. Changes in market trends.

5. Changes in corporate objectives, policies or management.

It is therefore **very difficult to put together an accurate list of banks which are aggressive in their issuance of credit cards. The list would become outdated and obsolete very quickly.**

So, how do we find banks which are aggressively seeking to issue credit cards? Simple! Find three or four friends, neighbors, or relatives with a long history of impeccable credit. People with good credit are always bombarded with credit card requests, many with pre-approved credit. (Credit card companies which do not offer similar products or services often exchange or sell mailing lists of good customers). When they do receive such requests, have them give you the name and address of the bank.

Additionally, be on the lookout for aggressive general advertising by these banks on T.V., radio or in print.

The above not only applies to banks but also to Travel & Entertainment Cards, Seller Credit Cards, and Debit Cards.

Secured Credit Cards

A secured credit card is issued because money that the cardholder deposits (C.D. or passbook) with the card issuing institution (bank or Savings & Loan) acts (is used) as security for any charge (balance) incurred on the card. The funds are frozen by the institution and are unaccessible by the cardholder until the arrangement is terminated (card returned to the institution). Most issuing institutions will give you only a percentage of the deposited amount as a credit line (total amount you can owe on the card). This amount in many instances is 50% (for example, if you had $2,500 deposited, your credit line would only be $1,250). The reason for this is that the possibility of a loss is not totally eliminated with a dollar for dollar deposit. It is possible to charge on a credit card more than your credit limit; therefore, most banks like having a "cushion" to protect themselves.

For example, assume an individual has a secured credit card with a $1,000 deposit and a 50% ($500) line of credit (amount he can spend). Merchants are only required to phone in to the credit card company for authorization/verification number (which is written in the slip) on any amount being purchased over a pre-stated amount (usually $50-$75). With amounts less than the pre-agreed upon call-in limit (let's assume $75) the merchant is only required to look in a monthly or bi-weekly credit card update for the authorization/verification number and/or to see if the card is valid. (However, he can still call it in if he chooses, but most will not). Assume an individual with a $500 line of credit (amount he can spend) chooses to purchase a television costing $400. He gives his card to the clerk who calls and receives an authorization code from the credit card company. What the credit card company does is set aside or freeze the $400 from his $500 limit. If the purchase had been $501, the merchant would have been immediately advised by the credit card company that the card had been denied. The individual still has a $100 line of credit he can spend ($500 – $400 TV purchase = $100 still available).

As previously discussed, if the individual were to make purchases under $75, the clerk would only have to look at his monthly or bi-weekly update to see if the card is valid. As you can see, the individual could make several purchases under $75 and very quickly be over its remaining $100 limit.

You can see now why banks are justified in only giving a partial line of credit on a deposit being held as security. Be sure and shop around, because some banks are now offering the same credit line for the same money deposited for savings. The number of banks issuing secured credit cards may be small now, but it is growing fast. Later in this section, we offer a list of banks currently offering this program.

Some banks, even with a deposit, may not accept some applicants with current credit problems, pending judgements against credit charge offs, or recent bankruptcy filing. Therefore, it is important to always inquire as to the bank's requirements before applying. Other banks will allow credit problems such as those mentioned above, but only mandate that they are at least twelve (12) months old. So, if one bank says no, don't give up!

Secured credit cards should only be sought if all other efforts to obtain an unsecured card have failed. Secured credit cards have no benefits over unsecured, even though some institutions may offer lower interest rates (finance charges). Remember, your deposit is usually offsetting this lower interest rate.

Needless to say, secured credit cards, because of the greater security to the issuing institution, are much easier to obtain than unsecured. They are, however, a "stepping stone" to establishing or re-establishing credit.

How to Apply for a Credit Card

Applying for a credit card is like applying for any other loan. Some of the important things to remember are:

1. Select your bank and bankers wisely. Look for banks and bankers aggressively looking for your business. If the bank you patronize does not fall into this category, move your business elsewhere.

2. Find out what credit underwriting requirements the bank has. This can be done by simply sitting down with the loan officer and asking.

3. Before submitting, be sure to compute your debt to income ratio. This is done by adding all your monthly expenses and dividing this amount by your monthly income. Most banks will not approve you if this amount is over 50%.

4. Always list a checking and savings account on your credit card application, even if you only have small balances.

5. Fill in as much information as possible on the credit application.

6. Always write neatly (type if possible).

7. Only apply at one bank at a time. In this way, if you are rejected for credit, you will know what needs to be corrected, and you will not make the same mistake twice.

8. Make sure your credit report is accurate.

9. Make sure the telephone is listed in the applicant's name.

10. If this is your first credit card, ask for a small line of credit. You can always increase your limit later.

The Cost of Credit (Buyer Beware)
Credit Card Finance Charge Calculations

Adjusted balance method

Under this method, the finance charge is levied against the remaining balance at the end of the billing period. Interest charges on purchases made during the month are not calculated until the end of the next billing period. **This is the method least expensive to the cardholder.**

Average daily balance method

Most popular method in use today. Calculated by taking the previous billing balance and subtracting any payment received. Depending on the plan, new purchases may or may not be included. The creditors add your balances for each day in the billing cycle and then divide that total by the number of days in the cycle.

Previous balance method

Under this method, the finance charge is levied on the entire billing balance and does not take into consideration any payment made until the following month (billing cycle).

Under the Truth in Lending Act, all credit card issuing institutions are required to disclose the method of finance charge calculation in addition to the annual percentage rate (A.P.R.).

Two-cycle average daily balance method

Creditors use the average daily balances for two billing cycles to compute your finance charge.

Buyer Beware!

Be aware that the amount of the finance charge may very considerably depending on the method used, even for the same pattern of purchases and payments.

Valuable Facts About Credit Card Use

- Keep your credit cards in a safe place.

- Sign your card immediately upon arrival.

- The fewer the credit cards you own, the better; use them as a convenience, not for financing.

- Notify the credit card companies of any change in address.

- In case of theft, notify the credit card company immediately.

- Always reconcile your credit card account.

- Pay off all balances in full at the end of the month.

- Keep all information on credit cards in a safe place (card number, expiration date, phone number and address of issuing company) in case they are lost or stolen.

- Never sign a blank receipt.

- Save all of your receipts.

- Always destroy your carbons.

- Do not lend your credit cards to anyone.

- Avoid giving your credit card number over the phone if you are uncertain with whom you are dealing.

Closing Costs
(Important Information Needed Before Buying)

A house is probably the single largest credit purchase for most consumers, and one of the most complicated. The Real Estate Procedures Act, like the Truth in Lending Act, is also a disclosure law. The Act, administered by the Department of Housing & Urban Development, requires the lender to give you, in advance, certain information about the costs you will pay when you close the loan. This law helps you to shop for the lowest settlement costs available. To find out more about it, write to:

> Assistant Secretary for Housing,
> Office of Insured Single Family Housing
> ATTN: RESPA
> U. S. Department of Housing & Urban Development
> 451 7th Street S.W.
> Room 9266
> Washington D.C. 20410.

How to Obtain a Secured Credit Card

It is very difficult to put together an accurate list of banks who may be actively involved at all times in a secured credit card program. Banks who today may have certain policies or requirements may differ the following month as to certain programs. But be assured that there are banks (especially small and medium banks) that are very receptive. Always check with your local bank first; not only will they tend to be more lenient toward someone they have a history with, but it will instill a spirit of cooperation for further loans or services you may be trying to procure from them in the future.

Some of the banks may require you to open a savings account in their bank. For example, if you want a credit limit of $300 on your credit card you may be asked to put $500 or $600 into an interest bearing savings account. Once you have established good credit with your credit cards, you will be able to withdraw the original amount you invested plus any accrued interest. You may even get your credit limit raised on your credit card if you have demonstrated a good repayment history.

Still other banks may require you to fulfil what is called a time deposit account for an initial term. This means you are not allowed to withdraw from the security deposit account until a specific time has elapsed. That is why you would be better to initially contact those institutions closest to you.

How can you qualify for a credit card if you have no credit history? Who will take a chance on you if you once got into financial trouble? Where can you find a card with a much lower interest rate than you're paying now?

All three concerns can be addressed with a "secured" credit card. You put up cash; the lender gives you credit guaranteed by that cash. Here are several institutions with different kinds of programs that you might want to check:

- Key Federal Savings Bank (626 Revolution Street, Havre de Grace, MD 21078). Key Federal gives many people with prior credit problems a second chance. By putting up a minimum of $500, you can get a credit card with a $500 limit. The more you deposit, the higher your credit limit can be, up to a maximum of $5,000. There are no annual fees, application fees, processing fees or fees for cash advances.

- United Credit Network, Inc (8306 Wilshire Blvd., Suite 19, Beverly Hills, CA 90211; phone (213) 549-9669) Offers MasterCard® and Visa®. Fee is $35.00 annually.

- American National Bank of New York (Box C, Fleischmanns, New York, NY 12430). Here is a small bank ($40 million in deposits) with a big idea: It offers super-low interest rates – 2 percentage points over prime – to people who will secure his or her line of credit with a cash deposit.

  You can keep the money in a certificate of deposit or money-market account, whichever you prefer.

For a minimum of $1,000, you can get a credit line of $750. If you put up $2,500, your credit limit would be $2,250. The money on deposit guarantees your payments on your credit-card debt.

- The State Street Bank and Trust of Boston (225 Franklin Street, Boston, MA 02110). This bank is hunting for squeaky-clean borrowers who are willing to trade collateral for a lower interest rate.

  State Street's normal credit card rate is 16.5 percent. But if you open a home-equity line of credit, and set aside a portion of your home's value to secure a Gold MasterCard®, you'll be charged only 12.5 percent on the card (plus a $50 annual fee).

  The credit card and the home-equity line are two separate accounts.

Once you have a bank card, getting more like it is simple. To receive additional cards, keep in mind two rules.

First, never apply for a second card from the same bank where you already have a card. Go to a different bank offering the same kind of bank card.

Second, never use the same kind of bank card for a credit reference on the application for an additional card. Even different banks would rather you didn't have another of the same kind of card. It splits up their profits. But it's not illegal or even unethical to have two. And I've never known a bank to check you for additional cards.

After your research is completed in your home town, check out of state sources as well. It is important to note that when requesting credit card information with out of state banks, you should first ask if they accept national applications. This will save you future aggravation if their policy only permits local residents to apply.

Use the Bank's Money to Obtain a Secured Credit Card and Establish Credit

One reason why more people don't get secured credit cards to re-establish their credit is that they may be operating so close to the wire that it is difficult to leave even as little as $300 on deposit for any length of time. If that's your problem, here's your strategy: Make your deposit, let's say $500, in an interest-bearing account at the bank that issues your secured credit card, and when you get the card, go to any MasterCard® or Visa® bank and borrow back the money up to your limit. When you have a $500 deposit at a secured credit card bank, which has given you a $500 credit limit, you can borrow back the entire amount. Therefore, your $500 is tied up for only a month or so. The real interest you pay for the loan is only the difference between what you're being charged in interest by the bank and what you're being paid in interest for your deposit.

Secured Credit Card Sources

ISSUER	APR	FEE	PHONE	MIN. DEPOSIT
Arkansas Federal/ Charles J. Givens Organization	11.98%	$55	900-535-9800[1] ext. 401	$300
Savings Industrial Bank	14.90%	$20	800-779-8472	$500
First Trade Union Savings	15.00%	$25	800-242-0273	$500
First Interstate	18.00%	$35	800-825-8472	$250
First Consumers	18.90%	$20	800-876-3262	$400
New Era Bank	18.99%	$30	800-262-3610	$500
Suburban National	18.99%	$35	302-322-4305	$500
American National Bank of New York	19.80%	$69	800-234-8472	$500

(interest rates subject to change)

[1] Call costs $2.00 for first minute, $1.00 per minute thereafter.

Lowest Interest Credit Card Sources
(With Annual Fees)

Name of Bank/Org.	Interest Rates	Card Type	National App.s	Out of State	Grace Period
Arkansas Federal/ Givens Organization P. O. Box 3111 Orlando, FL 32802 (800) 284-4082	8.25 (Fixed)	Visa/MC	$37.50	Yes	25 days
First Tennessee Credit Card Center P. O. Box 1545 Memphis, TN 38101 (800) 234-2340	10.50 (Fixed)	Visa Gold	$35.00	Yes	25 days
People's Bank P. O. Box 637 Bridgeport, CT 06601 (800) 426-1114	11.50 (Fixed)	Visa/MC MC Gold	$25.00 $40.00	Yes Yes	25 days 25 days

continued on next page…

Lowest Interest Credit Card Sources (With Annual Fees)
Continued

Name of Bank/Org.	Interest Rates	Card Type	National App.s	Out of State	Grace Period
Ohio Savings Credit Card Dept. P. O. Box 94712 Cleveland, OH 44114 (800) 962-2025	14.75 (Fixed)	Visa/MC Visa/MC Gold	$25.00 $45.00	Yes Yes	25 days 25 days
Wachovia Bank Card Svcs. P. O. Box 12264 Wilmington, DE 19850 (800) 842-3262	14.98 fixed or 9.4 variable	Visa/MC Visa/MC	$39.00 $25.00	Yes Yes	25 days 25 days
Arkansas Federal Savings Credit Card Center P. O. Box 8208 Little Rock, AR 72221 (800) 477-3348	8.50 (Variable)	Visa/MC	$35.00	Yes	0
Bank of Hawaii Bank Card Center P. O. Box 1999 Honolulu, HI 96805 (808) 543-9611	16.5 fixed 12.6 variable	Visa Visa Gold	$15.00 $45.00	Yes Yes	25 days 25 days
Bank of Montana System P. O. Box 5023 Great Falls, MO 59403 (800) 735-5536	12.25 (Variable)	Visa/MC	$19.00	Yes	25 days
Bank One, Cleveland, N.A. 30 So. Park Place Painesville, OH 44077 (800) 395-0010	13.20 (Variable)	MC	$20.00	Yes	25 days
Bank One, Columbus, N.A. Bankcard Associates 1000 N. Market Street Milwaukee, WI 53201 (800) 388-0225	13.90 (Fixed)	Visa/MC	$25.00	Yes	25 days

continued on next page...

Lowest Interest Credit Card Sources (With Annual Fees)
Continued

Name of Bank/Org.	Interest Rates	Card Type	National App.s	Out of State	Grace Period
Crestar Bank P. O. Box 27122 Richmond, VA 23261 (800) 368-7700	15.90 (Fixed)	Visa/MC Visa Gold	$20.00 $35.00	Yes Yes	25 days 25 days
First National Bank of Omaha P. O. Box 3331 Omaha, NE 68103 (800) 688-7070	14.90 (Variable)	Visa/MC	$20.00	Yes	25 days
Simmons First National Bank Card Center P. O. Box 6609 Pine Bluff, AR 71611 (501) 541-1304	8.50 (Variable)	Visa/MC MC Gold	$25 in-st. $35 out-st.	Yes Yes	25 days 25 days
United Missouri Bank 921 Walnut Kansas City, MO 64106 (816) 471-6575	14.50 (Variable)	Visa/MC	$20.00	Yes	25 days
First Signature Bank & Trust 190 Commerce Way P. O. Box 7090 Portsmouth, NH 03801-7090 (800) 522-1776	15.74 (Variable)	Visa	$20.00	Yes	25 days
First National Bank Greatbank Card Services P. O. Box 403 Chicago Heights, IL 60411 (208) 754-3202	15.96 (Fixed)	Visa/MC	$15.00	Yes	25 days

Lowest Interest Credit Card Sources
(No Annual Fees)

Name of Bank/Org.	Interest Rates	Card Type	Yearly Fees	National Apps.	Grace Period
Star Bank Card Services Group P. O. Box 956 Cincinnati, OH 45201 (800) 999-0619	14.00 (Variable)	Visa/MC	None	OH, IN, KY, WY	0
Horizon Savings Box 9600 Austin, TX 78767 (800) 289-2733	15.10 (Fixed)	Visa/MC	None	Yes	25 days
USAA Federal Savings Bank Card Center P. O. Box 21658 Tulsa, OK 74121 (800) 922-9092	13.75 (Variable)	Visa/MC	None	Yes	25 days
Manufacturer's Bank – Wilmington P. O. Box 15147 Wilmington, DE 19885 (800) 635-8350	14.80 (Fixed)	Visa/MC	None	MI, OH, IL, WI, FL, MN	0
Union Planters Bank P. O. Box 1167 Memphis, TN 38103-1167 (800) 628-8946	15.25 13.50 (Fixed)	Memphis Visa MC Gold	None None	Yes Yes	0 25 days
Oak Brook Bank P. O. Box 5033 Oak Brook, IL 60522 (800) 666-1011	16.80 (Fixed)	MC Gold	None	Yes	25 days
Bank of New York (Delaware) P. O. Box 6999 Newark, DE 19714 (800) 942-1977	11.90 (Fixed)	Visa/MC	None	Yes	0
Abbott Bank 10040 Regency Circle Suite 300 Omaha, NE 68114 (800) 999-6977	16.30 (Fixed)	Visa/MC	None	Yes	25 days

continued...

Lowest Interest Credit Card Sources (No Annual Fees)
Continued

Name of Bank/Org.	Interest Rates	Card Type	Yearly Fees	National Apps.	Grace Period
AFBA Industrial Bank KBC Card Services 909 N. Washington St. Alexandria, VA 22314 (800) 776-2265	12.50 (Fixed)	Visa/MC	None	Yes	25 days
Amalgamated Bank of Chicago Card Services Dept. 1 West Monroe St. Chicago, IL 60603 (800) 365-6464	12.50 11.00 (both variable)	MC MC Gold	None None	Yes Yes	25 days 25 days

(all information is deemed accurate, but not guaranteed — subject to change)

Multiple Credit Card Acquisitions

In recent months many self proclaimed credit experts have been advising their clients to acquire dozens and even hundreds of bank credit cards. The purpose of acquiring all these cards is to have a large unsecured line of credit available to the consumer. For example, if the consumer had 50 Visa® cards with a $1,000 line of credit on each, he could walk into a bank and get a total of $50,000 in cash. These funds in turn are used to make "investments" which are quickly liquidated. Many of these "experts" are even using the number of cards they personally acquire as a demonstration of their ability. However, it is strongly advised **not** to participate in this type of financing. Acquiring multiple credit cards simply entails applying at several banks at once and always maintaining a zero balance on the credit cards already obtained in order to fraudulently **not** list them as a contingent liability on the application. When a bank approves a customer for a 30 or 40 thousand dollar unsecured line of credit, they take into consideration a number of factors: namely his ability to repay, regardless of what happens to the 30 or 40 thousand dollars; his experience in the use of the funds; and the intended use of the funds. With few exceptions, most people who are acquiring multiple credit cards from multiple banks do not have the ability to repay the funds if they were lost on a bad investment (no to mention, pocket the money and **think** he can walk away); nor do they have the experience to differentiate between a good and an excellent investment (inexperiences and unsophisticated). Also, bank credit cards are issued with the intention of granting the consumer a purchasing convenience and not as a catalyst of a get-rich-quick scheme.

If a consumer were to lose several thousand dollars, even if his intentions were good, and could not repay, the banks could feel they were the victim of a fraud, and criminal prosecution could be a reality.

In any case, it spells trouble for everyone involved. Stay away from this type of "financing".

Note: The same principle also applies to multiple unsecured loans at different banks; the end result is the same – Trouble.

Consumer Rights Concerning Prompt Crediting and Billing

Some creditors will not charge a finance charge if you pay your account within a certain grace period. In this case, it is especially important that you get your bills, and get credit for paying them promptly. Check you statements to make sure your creditor follows these rules:

Prompt Billing: Look at the date on the postmark. If your account is one on which no finance charge is added before a certain due date, then creditors **must** mail their statements fourteen (14) days before payment is due.

Prompt Crediting: Look at the payment date entered on the statement. Creditors **must** credit payments on the day they arrive, not when someone gets around to posting it!

Credit Balances: If a credit balance results on your account (for example, because you pay more or you return a purchase) the creditor **must** make a refund to you within seven **business** days after your written request, or automatically if the credit balance is still in existence after six months.

Consumer's Name
Address
City/State/Zip

Date

Name of Bank
Street Address of Bank
City/State/Zip

Dear Sirs:

At your first opportunity, please forward me any available information and requirements, including an application, for a secured credit card (Visa, MasterCard).

Please specify your savings account or Certificate of Deposit requirements.

Thank you,,
(Signature)
Name

TITLE III – FAIR CREDIT BILLING ACT

§301. Short title

This title may be cited as the "Fair Credit Billing Act".

§302. Declaration of purpose

The last sentence of section 102 of the Truth in Lending Act (15 U.S.C. 1601)[36] is amended by striking out the period and inserting in lieu thereof a comma and the following: "and to protect the consumer against inaccurate and unfair credit billing and credit card practices."

§303. Definitions of creditor and open end credit and credit plan

The first sentence of section 103(f) of the Truth in Lending Act (15 U.S.C. 1502(f))[37] is amended to read as follows: "The term 'creditor' refers only to creditors who regularly extend, or arrange for the extension of, credit which is payable by agreement in more than four installments or for which the payment of a finance charge is or may be required, whether in connection with loans, sales of property or services, or otherwise. For the purposes of the requirements imposed under Chapter 4 and sections 127(a)(6), 127(a)(7), 127(a)(8), 127(b)(1), 127(b)(2), 127(b)(3), 127(b)(9), and 127(b)(11) of Chapter 2 of this Title, the term 'creditor' shall also include card issuers whether or not the amount due is payable by agreement in more than four installments or the payment of a finance charge is or may be required, and the Board shall, by regulation, apply these requirements to such card issuers, to the extent appropriate, even though the requirements are by their terms applicable only to creditors offering open end credit plans.

§304. Disclosure of fair credit billing rights

(a) Section 127(a) of the Truth in Lending Act (15 U.S.C. 1637(a))[38] is amended by adding at the end thereof a new paragraph as follows:

> "(8) A statement, in a form prescribed by regulations of the Board of the protection provided by sections 161 and 170 to an obligor and the creditor's responsibilities under sections 162 and 170. With respect to each of two bililng cycles per year, at semiannual intervals, the creditor shall transmit such statement to each obligor to whom the creditor is required to transmit a statement pursuant to section 127(b) for such billing cycle."

(b) Section 127(c) of such Act (15 U.S.C. 1637(c))[39] is amended to read:

> "(c) In the case of any existing account under an open end consumer credit plan having an outstanding balance of more than $1 at or after the close of the creditor's first full billing cycle under the plan after the effective date of subsection (a) or any amendments thereto, the items described in subsection (a), to the extent applicable and not previously disclosed, shall be disclosed in a

notice mailed or delivered to the obligor not later than the time of mailing the next statement required by subsection (b)."

§305. Disclosure of billing contact

Section 127(b) of the Truth in Lending Act (15 U.S.C. 1637(b))[40] is amended by adding at the end thereof a new paragraph as follows:

"(11) The address to be used by the creditor for the purpose of receiving billing inquiries from the obligor."

§306. Billing practices

The Truth in Lending Act (15 U.S.C. 1601 - 1665)[41] is amended by adding at the end thereof a new chapter as follows:

"Chapter 4 – Credit Billing"

"Sec.
"161.   Correction of billing errors.
"162.   Regulation of credit reports.
"163.   Length of bililng period.
"164.   Prompt crediting of payments.
"165.   Crediting excess payments.
"166.   Prompt notification of returns.
"167.   Use of cash discounts.
"168.   Prohibition of tie-in services.
"169.   Prohibition of offsets.
"170.   Rights of credit card customers.
"171.   Relation to State laws.

"§161. Correction of billing errors

"(a) If a creditor, within sixty days after having transmitted to an obligor a statement of the obligor's account in connection with an extension of consumer credit, receives at the address disclosed under section 127(b)(11) a written notice (other than notice on a payment stub or other payment medium supplied by the creditor if the creditor so stipulates with the disclosure required under section 127(a)(8) from the obligor in which the obligor –

"(1) sets forth or otherwise enables the creditor to identify the name and account number (if any) of the obligor,

"(2) indicates the obligor's belief that the statement contains a billing error and the amount of such billing error, and

"(3) sets forth the reasons for the obligor's belief (to the extent applicable) that the statement contains a billing error,

the creditor shall, unless the obligor has, after giving such written notice and before the expiration of the time limits herein specified, agreed that the statement was correct –

"(A) not later than thirty days after the receipt of the notice, send a written acknowledgement thereof to the obligor, unless the action required in subparagraph (B) is taken within such thirty-day period, and

"(B) not later than two complete billing cycles of the creditor (in no event later than ninety days) after the receipt of the notice and prior to taking any action to collect the amount, or any part thereof, indicated by the obligor under paragraph (2) either –

"(i) make appropriate corrections in the account of the obligor, including the crediting of any fiannce charges on amounts erroneously billed, and transmit to the obligor a notification of such correction and the creditor's explanation of any change in the amount indicated by the obligor under paragraph (2) and, if any such change is made and the obligor so requests, copies of documentary evidence of the obligor's indebtedness; or

"(ii) send a written explanation or clarification to the obligor, after having conducted an investigation, setting forth to the extent applicable the reaons why the creditor believes the account of the obligor was correctly shown in the statement and, upon request of the obligor, provide copies of documentary evidence of the obligor's indebtedness. In the case of a billing error where the obligor alleges that the credito's bililng statement reflects goos not delivered to the obligor or his designee in accordance with the agreement made at the time of the transaction, a creditor may not consture such amount to be correctly shown unless he determines that such goods were actually delivered, mailed, or otherwise sent to the obligor and provides the obligor with a statement of such determination.

After complying with the provisions of this subsection with respect to an alleged billing error, a creditor has no further resopnsibility under this section if the obligor continues has no further responsibility under this section if the obligor continues to make substantially the same allegation with respect to such error.

"(b) For the purpose of this section, a 'billing error' consists of any of the following:

"(1) A reflection on a statement of an extension of credit which was not made to the obligor or, if made, was not in the amount reflected on such statement.

"(2) A reflection on a statement of an extension of credit for which the obligor requests additional clarification including documentary evidence thereof.

"(3) A reflection on a statement of goods or services not accepted by the obligor or his designee or not delivered to the obligor or his designee in accordance with the agreement made at the time of a transaction.

"(4) The creditor's failure to reflect properly on a statement a payment made by the obligor or a credit issued to the obligor.

"(5) A computation error or similar error of an accounting nature of the creditor on a statement.

"(6) Any other error described in regulations of the Board.

"(c) For the purposes of this section, 'action to collect the amount, or any part thereof, indicated by an obligor under paragraph (2) does not include the sending of statements of account to the obligor following written notice from the obligor as specified under subsection (a), if –

"(1) the obligor's account is not restricted or closed because of the failure of the obligor to pay the amount indicated under paragraph (2) of subsection (a), and

"(2) the creditor indicates the payment of such amount is not required pedning the creditor's compliance with this section.

Nothing in this section shall be construed to prohibit any action by a creditor to collect any amount which has not been indicated by the obligor to contain a billing error.

"(d) Pursuant to regulations of the Board, a creditor operating an open end consumer credit plan may not, prior to the sending of the written explanation or clarification required under paragraph (B)(ii), restrict or close an account with respect to which the obligor has indicated pursuant to subsection (a) that he believes such account to contain a billing error solely because of the obligor's failure to pay the amount indicated to be in error. Nothing in this subsection shall be deemed to prohibit a creditor from applying against the credit limit on the obligor's account the amount inicated to be in error.

"(e) Any creditor who fails to comply with the requirements of this section or section 162 forfeits any right to collect from the obligor the amount indicated by the obligor under paragraph (2) of subsection (a) of this section, and any finance charges thereon, except taht the amount required to be forfeited under this subsection may not exceed $50.

"§162. *Regulation of credit reports*

"(a) After receiving a notice from an obligor as provided in section 161(a), a creditor or his agent may not directly or indirectly threaten to report to any person adversely on the obligor's credit rating or credit standing because of the obligor's failure to pay the amount indicated by the obligor under section 151(a)(2), and such amount may not be reported as delinquent to any third party until the crditor has met the requirements of section 161 and has allowed the obligor the same number of days (not less than ten) thereafter to make payment as is provided under teh credit agreement with the obligor for the payment of undisputed amounts.

"(b) If a creditor receives a further written notice from an obligor that an amount is still in dispute within the time allowed for payment under subsection (a) of this section, a creditor may not report to any third party that the amount of the obligor is delinquent because the obligor has failed to pay an amount which he has indicated under section 161(a)(2), unless the creditor also reports that the amount is in dispute and, at the same time, notifies the obligor of the name and address of each party to whom the creditor is reporint information concerning the delinquency.

"(c) A creditor shall report any subsequent resolution of any delinquencies reported pursuant to subsection (b) to the parties to whom such delinquencies were intially reported.

"§163. *Length of bililng period.*

"(a) If an open end consumer credit plan provides a time period within which an obligor may repay any portion of the credit extended without incurring an additional finance charge, such additional finance charge may not be imposed with respect to such portion of the credit extended for the biling cycle of which such period is a part unless a statement which includes the amount upon which the finance charge for that period is based was mailed at least fourteen days prior to the date specified in the statement by which payment must be made in order to avoid imposition of that finance charge.

"(b) Subsection (a) does not apply in any case where a creditor has been prevented, delayed, or hindered in making timely mailing or delivery of such periodic statement within the time period specified in such subsection because of an act of God, war, natural disaster, strike, or other excusable or justifiable cause, as determined under regulations of the Board.

"§164. *Prompt crediting of payments*

"Payments received from an obligor under an open end consumer credit plan by the creditor shall be posted promptly to the obligor's account as specified in regulations of the Board. Such regulations shall prevent a finance charge from being imposed on any obligor if the creditor has received the obligor's payment in readily identifiable form in the amount, manner, location, and time indicated by the creditor to avoid the imposition thereof.

"§165. *Crediting excess payments*

"Whenever an obligor transmits funds to a creditor in excess of the total balance due on an open end consumer credit account, the creditor shall promptly (1) upon request of the obligor refund the amount of the overpayment, or (2) credit such amount to the obligor's account.

"§166. *Prompt notification of returns*

"With respect to any sales transaction where a credit card has been used to obtain credit, where the seller is a person other than the card issuer, and where the seller accepts or allows a return of the goods or forgiveness of a debit for services which were the subject of such sale, the seller shall promptly transmit to the credit card issuer, a credit statement with respect thereto and the credit card issuer shall credit the account of the obligor for the amount of the transaction.

"§167. Use of cash discounts

"(a) With respect to credit cards which may be used for extensions of credit in sales transactions in which the seller is a person other than the card issuer, the card issuer may not, by contract or otherwise, prohibit any such seller from offering a discount to a cardholder to induce the cardholder to pay by cash, check or similar means rather than use a credit card.

"(b) With respect to any sales transaction, any discount not in excess of 5 per centum offered by the seller for the purpose of inducing payment by cash, check, or other means not involving the use of a credit card shall not constitute a finance charge as determined under section 106, if such discount is offered to all prospective buyers and its availability is disclosed to all prospective buyers clearly and conspicuously in accordance with regulations of the Board.

"§168. Prohibition of tie-in service

"Notwithstanding any ageement to the contrary, a card issuer may not require a seller, as a conditi to participating in a credit card plan, to open an account with or procure any other service from the card issuer or its subsidiary or agent.

"§169. Prohibition of offsets

"(a) A card issuer may not take any action to offset a cardholder's indebtedness arising in connection with a consumer credit transaction under the relevant credit card plan against funds of the cardholder held on deposit with the card issuer unless –

"(1) such action was previuosly authorized in writing by the cardholder in accordance with a credit plan whereby the cardholder agrees periodically to pay debts incurred in his open end credit account by permitting the card issuer periodically to deduct all or a portion of such debt from the cardholder's deposit account, and

"(2) such action with respect to any outstanding disputed amount not be taken by the card issuer upon request of the cardholer.

In the case of any credit card account in existence on the effective date of this section, the previous written authorization referred to in clause (1) shall not be required until the date (after such effective date) when such account is renewed, but in no case later than one year after such effective date. Such written authorizatin shall be deemed to exist if the card issuer has previously notified the cardholder that the use of his credit card account will subject any funds which the card issuer holds in deposit accounts of such cardholder to offset against any amounts due and payable on his credit card account which have not been paid in accordance with the terms of the agreement between the card issuer and the cardholder.

"(b) This section does not alter or affect the right under State law of a card issuer to attach or otherwise levy upon funds of a cardholder held on deposit with the card issuer if that remedy is constitutionally available to creditors generally.

"§170. Rights of credit card customers

"(a) Subject to the limitation contined in subsection (b), a card issuer who has issued a credit card to a cardholder pursuant to an open end consumer credit plan shall be subject to all claims (other than tort claims) and dfenses arising out of any transaction in which the credit card is used as a method of payment or extension of credit if (1) the obligor has made a good faith attempt to obtain satisfactory resolution of a disagreement or problem relative to the transaction from the person honoring the credit card; (2) the amount of the intial transaction exceeds $50; and (3) the place where the intial transaction occurred was in the same State as the mailing address previously provided by the cardholder or was within 100 miles from such address, except that the limitations set forth in clauses (2) and (3) with respect to an obligor's right to assert claims and defenses against a card issuer shall not by applicable to any transaction in which the person honoring the credit card (A) is the same person as the card issuer, (B) is controlled by the card issuer, (C) is under direct or indirect common control with the card issuer, (D) is a franchised dealer in the card issuer's products or services, or (E) has obtained the order for such transaction through a mail solicitation made by or participated in by the card issuer in which the cardholder is solicited to enter into such a transaction by using the credit card issued by the card issuer.

"(b) The amount of claims or defenses asserted by the cardholder may not exceed the amount of credit outstanding with respeect to such transaction at the time the cardholder first notifies the card issuer or the person honoring the credit card of such claim or defense. For the purpose of determining the amount of credit outstanding in the preceding sentence, payments and credit to the cardholder's account are deemed to have been applied, in the order indicated, to the payment of: (1) late charges in the order of their entry to the account; (2) finance charges in order of their entry to the account; and (3) debits to the account other than those set forth above, in the order in which each debit entry to the account was made.

"§171. Relation to State laws

"(a) This chapter does not annul, alter, or affect, or exempt any person subject to the provisions of this chapter from complying with, the laws of any State with respect to credit billing practices, except to the extent that those laws are inconsistent with any provision of this chapter, and then only to the extent of the inconsistency. The Board is authorized to determine whether such inconsistencies exist. The Board may not determine that any State law is inconsistent with any provision of this chapter if the Board determines that such law gives greater protection to the consumer.

"(b) The Board shall by regulation exempt from the requirements of this chapter any class of credit transactions within any State if it determines that under the law of the State that class of transactions is subject to requirements substantially similar to those imposed under this chapter or that such law gives greater protection to the consumer, and that there is adequate provision for enforcement."

PART THREE:
ACQUIRING CREDIT

PART THREE: ACQUIRING CREDIT

Proper Methods In Establishing Credit

Establishing (or re-establishing) credit can be tricky. Essentially, what you are looking for is a lending insititution to "go on the hook" for you without the benefit of a track record (credit history). If the consumer had a history of having bad credit at one time, then he must be able to prove he has changed his ways. If the consumer is over 26 years old and has no credit history, many lenders will begin to wonder why… What could be wrong? Why hasn't someone given him credit before? Could he have a credit file/report under another address or name that is very derogatory? What have we failed to pick up on in his application? Therefore, in many instances, a younger person fresh out of college, trade or high school, may have an easier time establishing initial credit even though his salary may be less than the older person. All that will be discussed in the loan underwriting section applies more than ever to establihsing initial credit. But as previously discussed, the creditor has no historic infomraiton to base his judgement on, and this can be problematic.

Below are several ways and suggestions how to overcome this problem.

- Open a checking or savings account. These do not begin your credit file, but may be checked as evidence that you know how to manage money.

- Go to a major department store. Buy a large ticket item on lay-away. After doing this a few times, ask the credit manager for a credit card.

- Apply for department store and/or oil company cards first. Bankcards and Travel & Entertainment card requirements are stricter.

- Always ask for the smallest credit limit they have. Later on you can increase it, but for the meantime you have your foot in the door.

- If you don't qualify on the basis of your own credit rating, offer to have someone co-sign your application.

- Get a secured credit card. After making payments promptly for 18 months, ask them to release your security deposit. If they refuse, apply elsewhere.

- Get a secured loan, pledge a C.D. or passbook account as collateral; if you do not have the money, borrow it from a friend and with the proceeds from the loan, pay him back.

- If you are refused credit, talk to the credit manager and find out why. Ask the credit manager **what he would do if he were in your position.**

- Remember, you may have a lot of credit which does not appear on your credit report. Make the creditor aware of this by asking the unreporting creditor to give you a letter as to your payment history and submit it with your application (send a copy to the credit bureau to add to your credit file).

- **When you finally do receive credit, make all payments on time.**

How to Get A Car Loan Even if You Are Non-Financable

If the consumer is in need of a car, but his credit or the lack of it is preventing him from acquiring one, there are two immediate alternatives available to him: (a) many late model used car lots will finance their purchase for a short term ("buy here, pay here"), or (b) if the consumer needs or wants a new car, he should find a very large dealership. After negotiating price, he should ask to speak to the finance and insurance manager. Next, he should explain his position to the finance and insurance manager and ask him to take the loan on "recourse". Recourse means that the dealership will discount or sell the loan to a bank and guarantee the bank that in case the consumer were to default on the loan, the dealership would buy the loan back from the bank. This type of loan is essentially the same as getting a co-signer (as guarantor) except if the loan is reported to the credit bureua, **it will most likely not be recorded as a co-signed loan.** If this technique is used, usually a large down payment may be required and the interest rate will be high.

What Creditors Look For

Applying for credit, be it a credit card, car loan, or any other type of credit extension is underwritten (analyzed) in basically the same fashion.

The Four C's of Credit:

Character – is all the features, traits, and peculiarities of an individual which distinguishes one person from another. The lending institition is looking for an applicant's character to have the moral qualities to pay his obligation. Regardless of circumstances, this quality can be found in rich and poor alike. What the lending institution is trying to avoid is an individual with the necessary financial resources to repay a debt but an unwillingness to do so. How does the lender ascertain these qualities? In the case of a large loan, usually there is contact between the lender and applicant (telephone or in person), but in the case of most requests (i.e., credit cards, or a car loan through a car dealer or broker) where there is no contact, a credit report and purpose of loan is usually the only indication available to the lender.

Capital – or net worth, is the sum of the applicant's tangible assets expressed monetarily (estimated dollar value of items he owns) over his liabilities (dollar amounts that he owes). Net worth or capital is important to the lending institution because it permits them to know what else the applicant has available in case of financial duress. It also demonstrates stability and the resources available to the applicant to pay his debt. Net worth statement (or personal financial statements) are only required when trying to procure large loans such as a mortgage. They are seldom required for car loans, credit cards or smaller loans of this nature.

Capacity – is the ability of the borrower to procure enough income on a steady basis to pay his debt (can he afford the monthly payment?). Most people who buy large items cannot afford to pay for them in cash; therfore; they rely on current income received to discharge the debt over an extended period of time. In order for a loan transaction to be economically feasible to the lending institition, the borrower must be able to demonstrate his future earnings potential. One of the most important measures of capacity is the debt to income ratio. **Debt to income is calculated by totalling all monthly debt** (example: car payment, rent or mortgage, personal loans, alimony, etc.) **including the monthly payment of the proposed item to be financed and dividing it by the monthly income.** Most banks will not lend if the ratio is over 50%. It is important to ask the creditor what ratio they use. I have provided a sample bank Debt Service and Financing Worksheet; the debt to income ratio, among other things, is calculated here. This particular bank's debt to income ratio is 36% for applicants with incomes under $3,500 per month and 40% for applicants with incomes over $3,500 per month. Other items to measure the capacity are based on the stability of income. If a wife is a co-applicant, will she give up her job in the future to raise a family? If an applicant is submitting his application based on additional overtime income, how long will it last? Is the applicant's employer or industry stable? As you might conclude, the creditor has to be somewhat of an economist or fortune teller at times. Needless to say, the job is not easy.

Collateral – is an item of value pledged by the borrower to the lender as additional security for a loan. If the loan is for durable "goods" (example: house or car), the durable "good(s)" itself is pledged. If the consumer were to default, the item would be repossessed and sold by the lender. Hopefully, the collateral will be sold for at least the loan payoff amount. Payoff amount is the amound owed on a loan plus miscellaneous expenses incurred in the repossession and collection effort(s). If the amount brought in by the sale is not enough, the borrower is still responsible for the difference. For this reason, banks require a down payment on durable goods they finance; hopefully, the fair market value will be more than the loan payoff amount at any given time.

Credit Scoring System

In recent times, many bankers have tried to standardize credit analysis (especially on unsecured loans) by establishing a point system. In this system, a numeric value is assigned to different variables. The more favorable to the lender an item, the higher the number assigned. A point scoring system sample is provided; in this example, anything above 18 is passing, 15 - 17 is subject to review, anything below 15 is immediately rejected.

Credit Scoring System – Sample

CATEGORY	POINTS
Age Group:	
18 - 25	1
26 - 64	2
65 and up	1
Dependents:	
None	2
1 - 3	1
4 or more	0
Stability:	
Up to 5 years at present address	1
Over 5 years at present address	2
Years at Previous Address:	
Less than 5 years..	1
More than 5 years	2
Employment:	
Less than 1 year at present employment	1
1 - 3 years at present employment	2
4 - 6 years at present employment	3
7 - 10 years at present employment	4
Over 10 years at present employment.............................	5
Wife employed, if applying jointly	2
Telephone listed in applicant's name	2
Loan Experience:	
At bank where you are applying for loan........................	5
At another bank	3
Checking or Savings account at same bank....................	3
Checking or Savings account at another bank	2
Type of Work:	
Professional/Executive	4
Skilled worker...	3
Blue collar	2
All others	1
Monthly Obligations:	
Less than $250	2
More than $250	1

What Banks Consider To Be Negative Information

- No telephone number.

- Telephone not listed in applicant's name.

- New businesses.

- Unemployment at time of application.

- Employment with small, unknown (unstable) firm.

- Unskilled laborers.

- Glamour jobs that pay poorly.

- Enlisted military personnel.

- Self-employed people working out of their homes.

- Indians living on reservations.

- People of modest income with several revolving accounts, even if their present balance is zero.

- Drug addicts.

- Alcoholics.

- Minors.

- Frequent changes in employment.

- Frequent changes in address.

- Residence in hotels, boarding homes, etc.

- Using a Post Office box as an address.

- Co-applicants living together (unmarried).

- Non-constructive loans.

- High debt-to-income ratio.

- Convicted felons.

- Bankruptcies (Chapter 7)

- Wage Earner Plan (Bankruptcy – Chapter 13)

- Nationals of other countries without a "green card".

How To Improve Your Chances
Applying For A Loan

FIRST:

When you apply for a loan, your objective is to borrow money. There are, however, many ways to accomplish this. The first step in applying for a loan is to find the quickest, most convenient, inexpensive way to acquire your loan. For example, if you wish to take an extended vacation and you were to apply for an unsecured $5,000 loan, the loan officer might feel this is a waste of money. He may view it as an expense on an item with no lasting benefit. The fact that you have not had a vacation in five years or that you promised your wife is irrelevant to him. You may have been able to have solved your loan problem simply by applying for a MasterCard® Goldcard with a $5,000 limit, or, if you have one already, by having your limit raised. Mailing in the application or phoning to have your limit raised is much easier and convenient than having to go in person to a bank and "spill your guts" to a loan officer. The interest rate will probably be the same. The credit cards will have the advantage of a grace period and wil also be more convenient and safer.

SECOND:

Once you have found the most pracitical way of acquiring your funds, your second step is to find a lending institution and/or loan officer who is aggressively seeking that particular type of business. One of the first places to start is the bank that you patronize. Remember the credit scoring system (you are awarded more points if the loan is with the bank you currently do business with). Ask to speak to a loan officer and tell him what you are trying to accomplish. Be careful, **most lending officers are trained to remember what you tell them verbally.** If what you put on your credit application is different from what you told them, it will trigger a red flag. The idea of the interview is for you to get information and a credit application. Try to get answers to the following:

- What credit bureau(s) they belong to.

- Does the loan officer you are speaking with have the authority to grant the loan? If not, who does?

- The debt-to-income ratio that bank uses in calculating an applicant's capacity.

- How often they grant this type of loan.

- Interest rate and terms.

- Simple or add-on interest?

Under the Truth in Lending Act, Title I of The Consumer Credit Protection Act (it is strongly suggested that you read it; a copy is included in this handbook) all lending institutions are required to disclose to the consumer at least the following:

- What the Annual Percentage Rate is (APR).

- Length of the loan.

- The total cost of the loan in dollars if it is not pre-payed (monthly payment amount multiplied by the number of months).

- When the payments would be due.

- When the first payment would be due.

- What the penalty (late charge) is for a late payment.

- Any pre-payment penalties if the consumer choose to pay the loan off early.

- What collateral would have to be assigned to the loan, if any.

- The cost of other miscellaneous items such as credit life insurance.

THIRD:

Calculate your debt-to-income ratio. Is it too high? If so, you may need a co-applicant or co-signer. An interesting thing about salaries is that many banks do not bother to verify them as long as they appear reasonable for that particular line of work. If they do verify salary or credit history, it is always by phone or mail, and they have no idea who they are talking to or who is filling out the verification of employment form.

FOURTH:

Next, get your credit report (how to accomplish this was discussed earlier). If there are still any questionable items, write (type) a formal letter to the loan officer giving any additional explanation you deem appropriate along with your credit application.

FIFTH:

If the loan is for durable goods, and collateral is involved, make sure to have a good description of the item, along with a copy of the sales contract. If it's an item like a car, where there exists a value book (blue book), look up the item and make sure you are paying a fair price. This is most easily accomplished by asking your loan officer to look it up for you. This will also create an aura of working together, which is very important.

SIXTH:

Once you have completed the above, you are prepared to fill out the credit application. **Neatness in all paperwork cannot be over-emphasized.** If possible, type; if not print. Start out with the basic information – name, address, social securtiy number, etc. Banks like stability. Make sure your telephone is listed in your name. If you have moved several times in the past, this creates an illusion of instability. Be prepared to give an explanation, or better yet, you should reference the issue before the loan officer does. You can best do this by writing a footnote on the application, or with a formal letter, if it's a long explanation. For example, "Please be advised that I have lived at my Fairview address for over 10 years with my parents; however, when I went away to colege I was moved from dorm to dorm until finally I chose to live off campus. Now that I have graduated, I am back at my permanent address." College could be substituted with an enlistment in the armed forces or any other similar situation.

Make sure to have a savings and checking account, even if they have very small balances; it shows stability. Also, most banks do not bother to verify deposits, unless it is a large loan or mortgage, especially if the accounts are at other banks.

Next, list all loans and monthly obligations, even though the **only way a bank knows your monthly liabilities is from your credit report** (or if you list them in your application) – you should list them all. If no borrowing experience appears on your credit report, make sure to get letters from favorable creditors to supplement your credit application. Do not enclose your credit report with the loan application. Per policy, lending institutions are not allowed to use a credit report that has passed through your hands first.

Try to fill in as much as possible on the credit application. Don't be afraid to include a personal resume along with the application, or a cover letter. If you have little credit history, the more a bank knows about you, the better they'll feel (provided the information is favorable).

SEVENTH:

After you're through completing all of the above, look everything over. **Does all the information on the application concur with the central theme of the application?** In other words, does all the information on the application match the story you're telling?

Only apply at one institution at a time. This way, if you are turned down, you will know your weakness and can try to improve it when you appy elsewhere. When you submit your application, go in person if possible. The loan officer will review the application. If he asks any questions, make sure your answers concur with the information on the application. If the loan officer with which you are dealing has loan authority, he may approve it on the spot after running your credit report.

Bank officials play a funny game in trying to climb the corporate ladder. They seldom like critcism from their peers (colleagues trying to climb the same ladder) or from their superiors (persons they are trying to impress). Therefore, if the person you are dealing with has loan authority, he may give you the benefit of the doubt in certain gray areas. Your loan may be closed and funded quietly, whereas, if he had to confer with someone else in the bank, his choice might not be to give you the benefit of the doubt, for fear of losing status or prestige.

If you are turned down, try to talk to the person with loan authorization who turned you down (assuming you haven't been dealing with him up to now). Ask him what you can do to get approved, or better yet, ask "What would you do if you were in my shoes?".

AAA Credit In Thirty Days

Credit at a bank is the best credit. Use the bank's own money to establish your credit and earn a good credit rating at other banks also. Start with $400 ($200 if it's all you have). First, take the $400 to a bank and open a savings account. Wait three days for posting then apply for a $400 loan – offering your savings account for collateral. Since the loan is risk free the bank usually won't check your credit. If possible, deposit your money where they offer toasters, silverware or other valuable premiums.

Now you have $400 in the bank drawing interest and you have $400 in your hand.

The first $400 in the savings account is frozen, but that's not a problem. Take the second $400 (the borrowed money) to a second bank and open another savings account. Repeat the same procedure waiting three days again. Do this five times with five different banks (no more than five initially). After you have opened the savings accounts at the banks and obtained loans at each bank, take the last $400 from the last bank and open a checking account. Three days later you can begin repayment. Pay one full month payment on each loan, then one week later make another payment on each loan. At this rate you'll have all your loans repaid in about forty days. With each payment an equal amount of money will be unfrozen in your savings account, and that money can be placed in your checking account as you continue.

Whatever your former credit rating was, you now have not one, but five excellent credit references. After the first three early payments, your bank will automatically clear you for future signature loans at their banks and will give you a AAA-1 credit rating to anyone checking your credit rating.

Some hints:

- Always take your savings account book with you when applying for the loans since you will have to surrender it to the bank officer.

- Try to get a nine month repayment schedule for each loan even though you repay each loan much more quickly.

Your savings accounts will have earned some interest (small) which will offset some of the interest on the loans. You actually have paid a very small price for an excellent credit rating.

Now you are established and ready to apply for bank and credit cards. Since you have good credit with five banks you needn't worry about credit approval. Even Diner's Club® and American Express® should be no problem now. You should now be able to get an unsecured loan within twenty four hours.

Be sure you have carried out these instructions carefully; making the first deposit, getting the first loan, doing the same again and again and again. Be sure your payments are set up right, repaid before due time so you'll be ahead of schedule. All of this information must be carried out carefully if you want to establish that AAA credit rating.

A word of caution; do not use the same bank with five different branches. It must be five separate banks. And, check your local laws to be certain this program is applicable in your area.

Personal Budget Worksheet

Of paramount importance for every consumer to know exactly where and how his money is being spent. In this fashion, the consumer will be able to know where he can and cannot cut corners.

	PROJECTED	ACTUAL	DIFFERENCE
INCOME			
Salaries	$ _____	$ _____	$ _____
Wages from Self-employment	_____	_____	_____
Dividends	_____	_____	_____
Interest	_____	_____	_____
Rental Income	_____	_____	_____
Alimony Income	_____	_____	_____
Other Income	_____	_____	_____
TOTAL INCOME	$ _____	$ _____	$ _____
FIXED EXPENSES			
Food	$ _____	$ _____	$ _____
Housing	_____	_____	_____
Utilities	_____	_____	_____
Transportation	_____	_____	_____
Maintenance	_____	_____	_____
Furnishings	_____	_____	_____
Clothing	_____	_____	_____
Installment Purchases	_____	_____	_____
Personal Care	_____	_____	_____
Insurance Premiums	_____	_____	_____
Medical & Dental Care	_____	_____	_____
Education	_____	_____	_____
Taxes (Property, Federal, State & Local)	_____	_____	_____
Other Expenses	_____	_____	_____
TOTAL FIXED EXPENSES	$ _____	$ _____	$ _____
TOTAL AVAILABLE (Income - Fixed Expenses)	$ _____	$ _____	$ _____
VARIABLE EXPENSES			
Entertainment	$ _____	$ _____	$ _____
Recreation/Vacations	_____	_____	_____
Investments	_____	_____	_____
Savings	_____	_____	_____
Other	_____	_____	_____
TOTAL VARIABLE EXPENSES	$ _____	$ _____	$ _____
TOTAL AVAILABLE AT MONTH'S END	$ _____	$ _____	$ _____

SAMPLE: Cover Letter to accompany a request for a loan.

Consumer's Name
Address
City/State/Zip

Date

Bank Loan Officer
Bank or Loan Company Name
Street Address of Bank or Loan Company
City/State/Zip

Dear *Name of Bank Loan Officer*:

As per our conversation last week please find enclosed my credit application for a loan on a *(item being financed)*.

I have also included the following items which you indicated you would need in order to ascertain my credit worthiness.

– Copy of my current pay check/stub
– Sales Contract
– Copy of Title
– Proof of payment to *(name of creditor)* for an item incorrectly showing on my credit report.

I will call you in a few days after you have had a chance to review the enclosed. In the meantime, if you have any questions please don't hesitate to call me. Thanking you in advance for all your considerations,

Sincerely,
(Signature)
Name

Enclosure

Net Worth Worksheet

ASSETS	AMOUNT

Cash on hand $ _____

Savings and Checking Accounts
account number/bank

_____ $ _____
_____ $ _____
_____ $ _____

                         Subtotal (A) $ _____

Insurance Policies
account number/insurance company   cash value

_____ $ _____
_____ $ _____
_____ $ _____

                         Subtotal (B) $ _____

Securities & Bonds
account number/broker   value

_____ $ _____
_____ $ _____
_____ $ _____

                         Subtotal (C) $ _____

Real Estate
description   est. value

_____ $ _____
_____ $ _____

                         Subtotal (D) $ _____

Jewelry
account number/bank

_____ $ _____
_____ $ _____

                         Subtotal (E) $ _____

Automobiles
Year/Make/Model   est. value

_____ $ _____
_____ $ _____
_____ $ _____

                         Subtotal (F) $ _____

continued on next page…

Other Assets

description   est. value

_____ $ _____

_____ $ _____

_____ $ _____

                                   Subtotal (G) $ _____

        TOTAL ASSETS (Total of A through G) (H): $ _____

Liabilities/Debts

Creditor   Balance (amount owed)

(I) _____ $ _____

(J) _____ $ _____

(K)_____ $ _____

(L) _____ $ _____

(M) _____ $ _____

(N) _____ $ _____

        Total Liabilities (Total of I through N) (O) $ _____

                        Net Worth (H – O =) $ _____

Debt To Income & Financing Worksheet

Name of Applicant: _____ Co-Applicant: _____ Co-Signer: _____

Loan Amount: _____ Interest Rate: _____ Term: _____

---

1) Verifiable Gross Monthly Income

Applicant's Salary/Wages _____

Co-Applicant Salary/Wages _____

Co-Signer _____

Additional Monthly Income _____

_____ _____

_____ _____

_____ _____

Total Gross Mo. Revenue $_____(a)

Maximum Service Amount In $'s

If monthly income is $3,500 or less, go to line 2, if more, go to line 3.

2) Multiply by 0.36 $_____(b)
   (0.36 x amount on line A)

or multiply income in excess of $3,500:

3) Multiply by 0.40 $_____(b)
   (0.40 x amount on line A)

---

4) Total Monthly Fixed Expenses

Type of Account: Mo. Payment

_____ _____

_____ _____

_____ _____

* Any monthly payment amount not known can be estimated by multiplying original loan balance by 0.05

Mortgage or Rent Payment _____

Installment Loan _____

Other _____ _____

Other _____ _____

_____ _____

Misc. _____ _____

5) Total Current Fixed
   Monthly Expenses $_____
   (add all items in Section 4)

6) Proposed Loan
   Payment Amount $_____

7) Total Fixed Monthly
   Expenses inclusive of
   proposed loan. (add 5 & 6) $_____

TOTAL GROSS MONTHLY INCOME — TOTAL FIXED MO. EXPENSES = AVAILABLE INCOME

$ _____   —   _____   =   _____

     (fill in line 2 or 3)   Line 7   Line 8

Line 8 must be sufficient to meet other reasonable living expenses!

Downpayment Analysis

Collateral Description: _____

_____

Source of Value: _____

_____ + _____ = _____

  Loan Amount   Value   Percent of Financing

Loan Processor Initials:_____ ❑ Approved ❑ Loan Officer Initials: _____

                             ❑ Not Approved❑

SAMPLE: Credit confirmation letter.

To: _____   Date: _____
_____   Applicant: _____
_____   Address: _____
_____   City/St/Zip: _____
                                 Acct #: _____

Dear Sirs:

Please be advised that I have applied for credit to the financial institution listed below. I hereby authorize you to provide them all the requested information or any additional information they may require; either verbal or in written form.

Your cooperation is greatly appreciated.

Applicant's Signature

Original Amount – High Credit   _____

Origination Date   _____

Terms (months)   _____

Payment Amount   _____

Collateral   _____

Next Payment Due on What Date   _____

Date of Last Payment Received   _____

Present Balance Amount   _____

Rating or Payment Record (Choose One):

  ❏ Excellent   ❏ Very Good   ❏ Good   ❏ Average   ❏ Poor

Net Pay-Off Amount: $ _____ as of _____ per diem $ _____
                        amount owed   date   daily rate

Comments: _____
_____
_____
_____

By: _____ Title: _____ Date: _____

By: _____ (signature)

Mail To: _____
_____
_____

Women, Minorities and Credit

The Equal Credit Opporunity Act, Title VII of The Consumer Credit Protection Act, was originally inacted by Congress in order to try to eliminate discrimination against women involved in trying to procure credit. The act later expanded to include the prohibition of credit based on a person's race, color, place of natural origin, religion, sex, age, and marital status. Additionally, anyone who must exercise their rights under the act cannot be "blackballed" or "blacklisted" from being given a loan.

The Equal Credit Opportunity Act is a tremendous equalizer for women and minorities who may be trying to procure credit (especially for the first time). The Equal Credit Opportunity Act is a law which is truly in the spirit for which America stands. The only problem with it is that it is difficult for an applicant to prove he has been discriminated against since a credit rejection can be masqueraded with another, or several other reasons for credit refusal. Another problem is that the persons the Equal Opportunity Credit Act was designed to protect seldom exercise their rights under it. This is due, mainly, to five reasons:

- As previously explained, it is difficult to prove, since credit denials can be masqueraded with another reason. Therefore, the applicant may not even realize he has been a victim.

- Women may feel it is unlady-like to raise havoc.

- Many applicants are not aware that the law exists or how easy it is to file a complaint.

- The applicant may not want to get involved or compete in a white collar environment.

- Many applicants find it easier to apply elsewhere.

Under the Equal Credit Opportunity Act, creditors must consider the credit history of accounts women have held jointly with their husbands. Creditors must also look at the record of any account held only in the husband's name if a woman can show it also reflects her own creditworthiness. If the record is unfavorable – if an ex-husband was a bad credit risk – she can try to show that the record does not reflect her own reputation.

Summary of the Equal Credit Opportunity Act

- If your salary or income is enough to warrant the loan (adequate debt to income ratio), the lender cannot require you to get a co-signer or co-applicant.

- If you are a woman, you may use your maiden or married name, whichever you choose. You may even choose a combination of the names. The only restriction is that you cannot use your husband's name (For example, Mrs. David Smith would not be acceptable, since there may be another Mrs. David Smith if this is Mr. Smith's second marriage).

- The creditor has the right to inquire as to how many dependants you have in order to ascertain your spendable income, providing, of course, he requires this information from everyone. If you are a woman he cannot inquire as to your birth control practices or plans for parenthood.

- The creditor must take under consideration all income derived from alimony, child support, public assistance and part-time income. A woman is not required to reveal alimony and child support if she chooses not to. (If she chooses not to, then those amounts will not be taken into consideration when computing her debt to income ratio.) Also, a woman cannot be automatically rejected for credit if she lists her occupation as housewife.

- If there is a change in a woman's marital status (divorced, widowed, separated or chooses to legally change her name) the creditor cannot automatically require her to reapply for an existing loan. The only exception to this rule is if there appears to be a problem with a loan where a former husband's income had been taken into consideration at the time the loan was approved.

- A woman's marital status cannot be inquired into if she is trying to procure separate unsecured credit. The only exception to this is if the applicant lives in a community property State.

Community Property States:

- Arizona
- California
- Idaho
- Louisiana
- Montana

- Nevada
- New Mexico
- Texas
- Washington

Filing A Complaint If You Have Been Discriminated Against

If you think you have been discriminated against, cite the Law to the lender. If the lender still says no without a satisfactory explanation, you may file a formal complaint with the appropriate governmental agency listed below:

If your complaint is against a State Chartered Bank:

Director, Division of Consumer and Community Affairs
Board of Governors of the Federal Reserve System
Washington, D.C. 20551

If your complaint is against a National Bank:

Comptroller of the Currency, Consumer Affairs Division
Washington, D.C. 20219

If your complaint is against a Non-Member Insured Bank:

Federal Deposit Insurance Corporation
Office of Bank Customer Affairs
Washington, D.C. 20429

A sample letter is included.

If you choose to sue, you can sue up to $10,000 for actual damages, and up to $500,000 for a class action lawsuit. In a successful lawsuit, the court will also award you court costs and reasonable attorney's fees.

Consumer's Name
Address
City/State/Zip
Phone at Work
Phone at Home

Ref: Name of Bank
Address
City/State/Zip
Acct. # (if applicable)

Date

Appropriate Governmental Agency
Address

Dear Sir:

Please accept this letter as a formal complaint on the above referenced Bank. My complaint is as follows:

_____

_____

_____

_____

I have tried to resolve the above described problem directly with *name of bank,* but to no avail. The key person I dealt with was *name of person*.

I have enclosed photo copies of all pertinent paperwork to document my claims.

Sincerely,
(Signature)
Name

Enclosure

TITLE V—EQUAL CREDIT OPPORTUNITY

"§501. Short title

This title may be cited as the "Equal Credit Opportunity Act".

"§502. Findings and purpose

The Congress finds that there is a need to insure that the various financial institutions and other firms engaged in the extensions of credit exercise their responsibility to make credit available with fairness, impartiality, and without discrimination on the basis of sex or marital status. Economic stabilization would be enhanced and competition among the various financial institutions and other firms engaged in the extension of credit would be strengthened by an absence of discrimination on the basis of sex or marital status, as well as by the informed use of credit which Congress has heretofore sought to promote. It is the purpose of this Act to require that financial institutions and other firms engaged in the extension of credit make that credit equally available to all creditworthy customers without regard to sex or marital status.

"§503. Amendment to the Consumer Credit Protection Act

The Consumer Credit Protection Act (Public Law 90-321) ,63 is amended by adding at the end thereof a new title VII:

"TITLE VII—EQUAL CREDIT OPPORTUNITY

"Sec.
"701. Prohibited discrimination.
"702. Definitions.
"703. Regulations.
"704. Administrative enforcement.
"705. Relation to State laws.
"706. Civil liability.
"707. Effective date.

"§701. Prohibited discrimination

"(a) It shall be unlawful for any creditor to discriminate against any applicant on the basis of sex or marital status with respect to any aspect of a credit transaction.

"(b) An inquiry of marital status shall not constitute discrimination for purposes of this title if such inquiry is for the purpose of ascertaining the creditor's rights and remedies applicable to the particular extension of credit, and not to discriminate in a determination of creditworthiness.

"§702. Definitions

"(a) The definitions and rules of construction set forth in this section are applicable for the purposes of this title.

"(b) The term 'applicant' means any person who applies to a creditor directly for an extension, renewal, or continuation of credit, or applies to a creditor indirectly by use of an existing credit plan for an amount exceeding a previously established credit limit.

"(c) The term 'Board' refers to the Board of Governors of the Federal Reserve System.

"(d) The term 'credit' means the right granted by a creditor to a debtor to defer payment of debt or to incur debts and defer its payment or to purchase property or services and defer payment therefor. "

"(e) The term 'creditor' means any person who regularly extends. renews, or continues credit; any person who regularly arranges for the extension, renewal, or continuation of credit; or any assignee of an original creditor who participates in the decision to extend, renew, or continue credit.

"(f) The term 'person' means a natural person, a corporation, government or governmental subdivision or agency, trust, estate, partnership, cooperative, or association.

"(g) Any reference to any requirement imposed under this title or any provision thereof includes reference to the regulations of the Board under this title or the provision thereof in question.

"§703. Regulations

"The Board shall prescribe regulations to carry out the purposes of this title. These regulations may contain but are not limited to such classifications. differentiation, or other provision, and may provide for such adjustments and exceptions for any class of transactions, as in the judgment of the Board are necessary or proper to effectuate the purposes of this title, to prevent circumvention or evasion thereof, or to facilitate or substantiate compliance therewith. Such regulations shall be prescribed as soon as possible after the date of enactment of this Act, but in no event later than the effective date of this Act.

"§704. Administrative enforcement

"(a) Compliance with the requirements imposed under this title shall be enforced under:

"(l) Section 8 of the Federal Deposit Insurance Act, in the case of—

"(A) national banks, by the Comptroller of the Currency,

"(B) member banks of the Federal Reserve System (other than national banks), by the Board.

"(C) banks insured by the Federal Deposit Insurance Corporation (other than members of the Federal Reserve System), by the Board of Directors of the Federal Deposit Insurance Corporation.

"(2) Section 5(d) of the Home Owners' Loan Act of 1933. section 407 of the National Housing Act, and sections 6(i) and 17 of the Federal Home Loan Bank Act, by the Federal

Home Loan Bank Board (acting directly or through the Federal Savings and Loan Insurance Corporation), in the case of any institution subject to any of those provisions.

"(3) The Federal Credit Union Act, by the Administrator of the National Credit Union Administration with respect to any Federal Credit Union.

"(4) The Acts to regulate commerce, b,v the Interstate Commerce Commission with respect to any common carrier subject to **those Acts.** "

"(5) The Federal Aviation Act of 1958, by the Civil Aeronautics Board with respect to any air carrier or foreign air carrier subject to that Act. "

"(6) The Packers and Stockyards Act, 1921 (except as provided in section 406 of that Act). by the Secretary of Agriculture with respect to any activities subject to that Act. "

"(7) The Farm Credit Act of 1971. by the Farm Credit Administration with respect to any Federal land bank. Federal land bank association, Federal intermediate credit bank. and production credit association;

"(8) The Securities Exchange Act of 1934, by the Securities and Exchange Commission with respect to brokers and dealers and

"(9) The Small Business Investment Act of 1958. by the Small Business Administration, with respect to small business investment companies.

"(b) For the purpose of the exercise by any agency referred to in subsection (a) of its powers under any Act referred to in that subsection, a violation of any requirement imposed under this title shall be deemed to be a violation of a requirement imposed under that Act. In addition to its powers under any provision of law specifically referred to in subsection (a), each of the agencies referred to in that subsection may exercise for the purpose of enforcing compliance with any requirement imposed under this title. any other authority conferred on it by law. The exercise of the authorities of any of the agencies referred to in subsection (a) for the purpose of enforcing compliance with any requirement imposed under this title shall in no way preclude the exercise of such authorities for the purpose of enforcing compliance with any other provision of law not relating to the prohibition of discrimination on the basis of sex or marital status with respect to any aspect of a credit transaction.

"(c) Except to the extent that enforcement of the requirements imposed under this title is specifically committed to some other Government agency under subsection (a), the Federal Trade Commission shall enforce such requirements. For the purpose of the exercise by the Federal Trade Commission of its functions and powers under the Federal Trade Commission Act, a violation of any requirement imposed under this title shall be deemed a violation of a requirement imposed under that Act. All of the functions and powers of the Federal Trade Commission under the Federal Trade Commission Act are available to the Commission to enforce compliance by any person with the requirements imposed under this title. irrespective of whether that person is engaged in commerce or meets any other jurisdictional tests in the Federal Trade Commission Act.

"(d) The authority of the Board to issue regulations under this title does not impair the authority of any other agency designate in this section to make rules respecting its own procedures in enforcing compliance with requirements imposed under this title.

"§705. *Relation to State laws*

"(a) A request for the signature of both parties to a marriage for the purpose of creating a valid lien, passing clear title, waiving inchoate rights to property, or assigning earnings, shall not constitute discrimination under this title: *Provided, however,* That this provision shall not be construed to permit a creditor to take sex or marital status into account in connection with the evaluation of creditworthiness of any applicant.

"(b) Consideration or application of State property laws directly or indirectly affecting creditworthiness shall not constitute discrimination for purposes of this title.

"(c) Any provision of State law which prohibits the separate extension of consumer credit to each party to a marriage shall not apply in any case where each party to a marriage voluntarily applies for separate credit from the same creditor: *Provided,* That in any case where such a State law is so preempted, each party to the marriage shall be solely responsible for the debt so contracted.

"(d) When each party to a marriage separately and voluntarily applies for and obtains separate credit accounts with the same creditor, those accounts shall not be aggregated or otherwise combined for purposes of determining permissible finance charges or permissible loan ceilings under the laws of any State or of the United States. "

(e) Except as otherwise provided in this title, the applicant shall have the option of pursuing remedies under **the provisions of this** title in lieu of, but not in addition to, the remedies provided by the laws of any State or governmental subdivision relating to the prohibition of discrimination on the basis of sex or marital status with respect to any aspect of a credit transaction.

"§706. *Civil liability*

"(a) Any creditor who fails to comply with any requirement imposed under this title shall be liable to the aggrieved applicant in an amount equal to the sum of any actual damages sustained by such applicant acting either in an individual capacity or as a representative of a class. "(b) Any creditor who fails to comply with any requirement imposed under this title shall be liable to the aggrieved applicant for punitive damages in an amount not greater than $10,000, as determined by the court, in addition to any actual damages provided in section 706(a): *Provided, however,* That in pursuing the recovery allowed under this subsection, the applicant may proceed only in an individual capacity and not as a representative of a class.

"(c) Section 706(b) notwithstanding, any creditor who fails to comply with any requirement imposed under this title may be liable for punitive damages in the case of a class action in such amount as the court may allow, except that as to each member of the class no minimum recovery shall be applicable, and the total recovery in such action shall not exceed the lesser of $100,000 or 1 percent of the net worth of the creditor. In determining the amount of award in any classification , the court shall consider, among other irrelevant factors, the amount of any actual damages awarded, the frequency and persistence of failures of compliance by the creditor, the resources of the creditor. the number of persons adversely affected, and the extent to which the creditor's failure of compliance u as intentional.

"(d) When a creditor fails to comply with any requirement imposed under this title, an aggrieved applicant may institute a civil action for preventive relief, including an application for a permanent or temporary injunction, restraining order, or other action.

"(e) In the case of any successful action to enforce the foregoing liability, the costs of the action, together with a reasonable attorney's fee as determined by the court shall be added to any damages awarded b.by the court under the provisions of subsections (a), (b), and (c) of this section.

"(f) No provision of this title imposing any liability shall apply to any act done or omitted in good faith in conformity with any rule, regulation, or interpretation thereof by the Board, notwithstanding that after such act or omission has occurred, such rule, regulation, or interpretation is amended, rescinded, or determined by judicial or other authority to be invalid for any reason.

"(g) Without regard to the amount in controversy, any action under this title may be brought in any United States district court. or in any other court of competent jurisdiction, within one year from the date of the occurrence of the violation.

"§707. *Effective date*

"This title takes effect upon the expiration of one year after the date of its enactment.".

PART FOUR:
CREDIT COLLECTION

PART FOUR: CREDIT COLLECTIONS

Monthly Delinquencies

When a financial institution extends credit, they do so expecting prompt payment and compliance at all times with their terms and conditions. However, since this does not always happen, the lending or issuing institution (bank, Savings & Loan, department store, oil company, etc.) has certain in-house policies on how to handle such situations when they do arise. Described and outlined below is the general process most widely used by large institutions in trying to collect.

One month delinquent:

An account on which no payment has been received during the past (30 day) billing cycle. The initial contact will come in the form of a friendly reminder. This reminder is typically printed on the following month's (billing cycle) statement, or occasionally in a separate letter. Typically, most delinquencies are paid after this reminder. Most people who fall in this category do so because they forgot, or lost the statement (bill), or temporarily have no money.

Two months delinquent:

An account in which no payment has been received during the past two (30 day) billing cycles. At this point, the lending or issuing institution is still very interested in maintaining you as a customer, so they have to "walk a fine line". They need to collect, but do not want to scare, embarrass or intimidate you into not patronizing them. Usually, at this point, the consumer will receive several formal letters, typically 10 to 20 days apart in sequence. If no payment or response is received, the next step is a phone call. The topic of conversation will be the seriousness of delinquency and "is something wrong?"

Three months delinquent:

An account in which no payment has been received during the past three (30 day) billing cycles. At this point in time, the institution realizes they may have a serious problem (the longer the debt is overdue, the harder to collect) and will use all in-house means available to them (more letters and more phone calls) to collect prior to turning it over to a collection agency or attorney. In-house credit managers prefer not to do this for several reasons:

1. They lose a percentage of the amount owed (collection agencies receive as payment up to 80% of the amount recovered).

2. The in-house credit collection department may feel like someone else is doing their job.

3. Public relations considerations.

If, by this time, they have not done so already, the institution will rescind any credit you may still have available with them, and you will be advised that your account is being handed over to a collection agency or an attorney for collection.

More than three months delinquent:

An account in which no payment has been received during the past three (30 day) billing cycles and one day. At this time, the account is usually given to a third party for collection. If it's a very large financial institution, they may have a department set up to handle it themselves. In either case, they no longer have interest in maintaining you as a client. It is now "open season", and they plan to collect what is owed to them.

If the amounts are large, they are usually given directly to an attorney; if the amounts are small or more readily collectible, they are given to a collection agency first. If the collection agency is unsuccessful and the amount owed warrants it, it is given to an attorney for litigation.

Collection Agencies

Collection agencies are retained by a creditor when the creditor has abandoned you as a customer and feels he will not be able to collect the money owed to him. Collection Agencies are not interested in preserving goodwill; all they want to do is collect. Because collection agencies specialize in this function, they can go about it less expensively than credit departments.

Credit agencies will initiate their collection efforts with a formal letter. This letter advises the consumer that their account has been referred to them for collection and that you must pay (most people do at this time). During the next phase (if the consumer did not pay), the consumer will receive one or two more letters. The letters will be final demand/final notice letters. At this point, they will also start calling you on the telephone. Things can be said or insinuated on the telephone that collection agencies would not put in writing for fear of legal repercussion. The telephone is also very personal, and will have more effect than a letter. The collection agency will continue with a combination of telephone calls and letters to try to make you pay. Each effort will insinuate an escalation in the degrees of seriousness/repercussions for non-payment.

The Fair Debt Collection Practices Act In Summary

The Fair Debt Collection Practices Act was passed by Congress to set specific guidelines for third party collection agencies as to what they can and cannot do. The Act prohibits collection agencies from several outrageous collection techniques of the past. Collection agencies who have been found to violate the Fair Debt Collection Practices Act can be fined large amounts, up to $10,000 per day, for each violation. It is strongly suggested that you read the Fair Debt Collection Practices Act, Section 801 - 812 (elsewhere in this section).

The Federal Trade Commission is responsible for overseeing its enforcement. There are also state laws which parallel federal law; therefore, whenever filing a complaint with the Federal Trade Commission, a similar one should be filed with the attorney general of the State.

Under The Fair Debt Collection Practices Act, collection agencies cannot:

- Write to anyone other than yourself or your attorney/representative. They may, however, try to locate you by asking others as to your whereabouts if you have "skipped". But even to them, they cannot specifically disclose that they are trying to collect an unpaid bill from you.

- Use abusive/profane language or behavior – "to harass, oppress, or abuse any person" – to threaten violence or harm to property or reputation. Also, they cannot use the telephone to continually annoy; either by calling and hanging up, calling and not identifying themselves, or repeated calls.

- Call the consumer's home during inconvenient hours. They may only call during the hours of 8 a.m. to 9 p.m., unless the consumer specifically agrees otherwise. Also, they may not call the consumer more than twice a week.

- Advertise, publish or distribute a "deadbeat" list of consumers' names who owe money (also applies to verbally telling other people). This includes contacting the consumer by postcard or letterhead indicating the recipient owes money or that they are a collection agency.

- Make the consumer incur any expense for communicating with them (example: no collect calls).

- Contact you at your place of employment if your employer does not permit it.

- Use any fictitious name; this includes representing to be a law firm or any deceit involving misrepresenting themselves as a credit bureau, governmental agency, etc., both verbally or in writing. Also, the threat of arrest cannot be used.

- Ask the consumer for a post-dated check. Collection agencies at one time had a notorious reputation for convincing consumers to issue postdated checks "which would only be deposited when there were additional funds in the account". In actuality, the collection agency would immediately deposit the check and take funds that the consumer had earmarked for other purposes. Even though the check is postdated, and banks are not supposed to process them, many large banks, because of the tremendous volume of checks and/or careless tellers, will accept and process postdated checks.

  If the check does not "clear" and it "bounces", the collection agency is in a much stronger position than before. The consumer has written and issued a check knowing there were no funds in the account to cover it. This is a crime! Collection agencies can still accept postdated checks, but they are required to give the consumer a minimum of three days written notification that they are going to cash your check. . Additionally, all funds the consumer submits to a collection agency must be applied in the way they were agreed upon.

- Threaten to take legal action unless they plan to do so.

- Continue contacting the consumer after the consumer has specifically notified them to stop. At this point, the collection agency may only notify you one more time and their only alternative is to take legal action or forget the whole thing.

How To Avoid Collection Problems

The best way to avoid collection problems is to **always pay your bills on time!** If you cannot, then negotiate with the creditor before he gives it to a third party for collection or reports you late to the credit bureau. Remember, he still wants you as a customer. **Do not avoid the creditor,** he simply will not go away (unless the amount is *very* small). If your funds are limited and you are forced to make partial or inconsistent payments, remember, **not all creditors report to the bureau, so it is possible to be 90 days late on several accounts and still have your credit profile/ report indicate you are not in financial distress.** If you think or want to negotiate your debt, see sample settlement letters located elsewhere in this section.

How To Handle Collection Agencies

Collection agencies play a psychological game. The person calling the consumer is a very blunt individual who has heard every excuse imaginable. Collection agencies in general are wary of consumers who know their rights. They will avoid certain "gray" areas when trying to collect from these people.

If you are unable to avoid a dispute with a creditor, and he does give it to a collection agency, and they phone, the consumer should immediately:

1. Advise the collector he is aware of his rights.

2. Ask him for his name ("I assume this is your real name), his company's name (Collection agency), address, phone number and name of his supervisor.

3. Do not get upset or use profane language.

If the consumer chooses, he has the right to **ask the collection agency to verify the debt with the creditor.** The collection agency must do so within 30 days and send the consumer proof. Until the debt is verified, the collection agency cannot continue their collection efforts. This will delay the collection agency and force them to perform additional work. If you choose to advise the collection agency at any time to stop these collection efforts, they must do so. However, remember, the collection agency's only alternative is a lawsuit. The consumer should not do this unless he is willing and prepared to retain counsel and go to court.

It is important to realize that the collection agency works for the creditor and not vice versa. It is therefore strongly advised to **negotiate directly with the creditor if the consumer wishes to make a settlement.**

If a collection agency uses the telephone to harass a consumer, the consumer should call the telephone company and file a formal protest. If enough people do this, the telephone company may disconnect the collection agency's telephones. Without telephones, a collection agency will be like a carpenter without a hammer.

If the consumer feels the collection agency has violated his rights, he should, within thirty (30) days, file a formal complaint with the Federal Trade Commission (Federal regulatory authority) and the Attorney General of his state (State regulatory authority). If the consumer chooses to file a civil lawsuit, the action must be started within one (1) year of the violation.

Bankruptcy: Chapter 13 vs. Chapter 7

Bankruptcy is not a quick or easy solution to a consumer's financial or credit problems. Bankruptcies are the worst thing that can appear on someone's credit report. There are two types of bankruptcies: Chapter 7 and Chapter 13 (Wage Earner Plan).

CHAPTER 7 or STRAIGHT BANKRUPTCY

Chapter 7 bankruptcy is the complete elimination of all debts and assets (items of value) of the consumer (except those listed below). In a Chapter 7 bankruptcy almost all assets are forfeited in order to try to satisfy all outstanding auditors. Needles to say, there are never enough assets to cover all the outstanding debts (if there were, there would be no need to go bankrupt), so creditors usually end up losing a very large portion of the money owed to them.

The Constitution of the United Stated permits Congress to establish and maintain uniform bankruptcy laws. Straight bankruptcy stays on a consumer's report for ten and possibly up to fourteen years. Six (6) years must pass before a person is eligible to file again for another bankruptcy.

Debts not discharged with bankruptcy:

- Alimony

- Child support

- Federal Income Tax owed

- Any debt you omitted from your petition

- Penalties owed to the government

- Debts incurred from willful malice

- Any debt incurred by fraudulent means such as fraud, embezzlement, theft. It will also cover items bought with a credit card prior to filing, knowing full well you had no intention of paying for the item. Another example would be loans procured with false financial statements or a false tax return.

ITEMS TO CONSIDER BEFORE FILING FOR BANKRUPTCY

A. How will a bankruptcy being reported on your credit report for 10 years affect you.

   Analysis: Your credit may be so bad that it is beyond repair. Even though negative items stay on the credit report only seven (7) years as opposed to ten (10) for a bankruptcy, it might or might not be worth waiting the extra three (3) years.

B. How embarrassing will it be to you to have your entire financial history and spending habits revealed in court and to your creditors?

C. Morally, some people are compelled not to file, since deep down they realize they do owe the creditors.

D. Can you work your way out of this financial rut and not have to file for bankruptcy?

E. How deep in the hole should you be before realizing it is useless and decide to file?

   Analysis: It is suggested not to file if the amount you owe is less than the equivalent of one year net income and the cash equivalent of your possessions that would be included in the bankruptcy. For example, if a consumer has an annual net income of $20,000 and has $10,000 worth of property included in the bankruptcy, this would be a total of $30,000. This consumer should only file if he owes in excess of $30,000.

Debt Relief: Chapter 13, The Wage Earner Plan

If your debt situation is critical and requires immediate relief from all debts, large and small, you may want to consider filing a Wage Earner Plan.

The Wage Earner Plan is a Federal Law that is part of the Federal Bankruptcy Act. Rather than favoring the creditor, the 1978 Federal Bankruptcy Act actually favors individuals. Chapter 13 is a plan which provides relief from debts. This is done by consolidating your debts, substantially reducing them and sometimes even eliminating them.

WHO IS ELIGIBLE TO FILE FOR CHAPTER 13?

• The size of income isn't important; therefore, anyone can file Chapter 13 if they have a stable and regular income and make payments on a regular basis. The payments are set according to the Plan.

• Even those who have previously declared bankruptcy can file Chapter 13.

• You can file if you are self-employed in a small business – unless it is a corporation or partnership.

- If you are a small businessman with debts of up to $100,000 (unsecured) or with debts of less than $350,000 (secured), you may take advantage of the Plan.

- You may use the Plan even if your income is solely from Social Security, Veterans Administration benefits, a pension or unemployment.

- If two or more of the following situations fit you, then you are in what is referred to as a difficult debt situation and eligible for the Wage Earner Plan.

  - Are you forced to use credit cards to supplement you income?

  - Do you have a problem making your mortgage or rent payment?

  - Does 25% or more of your net monthly income go to pay installment bills?

  - Are you unable to save for emergencies?

- If you lose your job while on the Wage Earner Plan, or encounter money problems beyond your control, you may be completely discharged from you debts (hardship reasons).

There are no attorney fees. You can file a Wage Earner Plan yourself. Go to the United States District Court and tell the clerk you are seeking relief under the Wage Earner Plan and you wish to fill out the forms. Be sure you have a complete list of income and debts. After you have finished the forms, pay the small filing fee.

The Plan then turns your debts over to the Federal Court for supervision. The court arranges to pay those bills for you, within your budget, and the court uses that portion of your income which is over and above your monthly living expenses. However, the Plan must be budgeted within a five year period.

Once the Plan is in motion, a restraining order will be issued within in twenty-four hours of the time you filed the Plan. This restraining order will do three things:

1) Prevent harassment, threats or contact with you in any way by your creditors.

2) Stop legal action against you – there can be no garnishments, seizures or property attachments or assignments.

3) Prevent accruing interest, service charges and late payments.

Time is gained because you will not pay any money to any creditors for three months (pending the court date). The plan will provide these reliefs:

- Your credit rating will not be ruined or adversely affected.

- Payments are set up on a regular basis – monthly, weekly or whatever is convenient for you.

- Your payments are put in a comfortable range for you.

- Obligations of your co-signers are discharged.

- You can challenge charges or debts that you feel are unfair or questionable (this is under court supervision).

- If the creditor does not file a claim within six months after the court submits a payment plan to him, the Plan then discharges you from that debt (almost 40% of creditors fail to file that claim; therefore, almost half of your debts can be dismissed).

- Sometimes you can settle (under the new law) for less than you owe. You may return the collateral on a secured loan – if you wish. For example, if you want to return the car to the creditor, the bill is discharged.

Bankruptcy Chapter 7, Total Freedom From Debts

Use bankruptcy only as a last resort. Don't let creditors push you into a corner. Look into other possibilities before you use bankruptcy. In bankruptcy, creditors are allowed a fair share of your assets. When you file bankruptcy, all of your assets and debts are taken over by the court. Some are exempt and are given back to you (according to State law). Examples of exempt properties are your home (if home-steaded), clothing, necessary furniture and some personal belongings. Other properties are divided among creditors. In about 90% of the cases, the debtor pays less than $100 to his creditors. About 75% of debtors that file pay no reimbursement at all.

Bankruptcy is relatively simple and inexpensive. Bankruptcy papers can be purchased at stationery or office supply stores. Fill out the forms listing all of your debts. If you forget a creditor, you must pay him. Then list all of your assets, take the papers to the court house, pay a small fee and have the clerk or official file the bankruptcy for you.

When you are called to a hearing (usually in about sixty days), tell the court official that you are broke and cannot afford an attorney. Unless complicated procedures are necessary, the proceedings can usually be carried on without an attorney. Bankruptcy can then be affirmed.

Other Legal Strategies

For unmarried women...

Get married. After you are married, you can place your assets in your husband's name and protect their seizure.

For married men...

Transfer your assets to your wife. Assets in your wife's name cannot be seized because she is not legally responsible for your debt.

For married couples...

Move to a community property state. A husband's or wife's creditors cannot lay claim to the couple's community property. Community property states include Arizona, California, Idaho, Louisiana, Montana, Nevada, New Mexico, Texas and Washington.

Transfer assets to your small corporation...

Since corporations are legal entities, creditors cannot touch your assets once you have transferred these assets to the corporation. And, small corporations can be formed quite easily.

Homestead your house...

Homesteading is a very simple procedure that protects your home from creditors. This protection, however, is not automatic – you must apply. Just complete the necessary forms available in large stationary stores, get the forms notarized and file them at your county courthouse.

In bankruptcy proceedings, homestead property is exempt from creditors.

File a denial...

If you are served with a summons on a debt, it might be a good idea to file a General Denial. Without this General Denial, the creditor is almost assured of victory and the power to seize your assets.

A General Denial tells the creditor you are going to put up a fight. A legal fight can be long and expensive. Many times the collector will simply drop the lawsuit, especially if the debt is less than $500.

The procedure for filing a General Denial is simple. Go to the civil court clerk, and tell him you would like to file a General Denial. It's that easy.

Use the Uniform Commercial Code...

You can contend the contract is "unconscionable". That's just to say the contract is deceptive or tricky in language, has important sentences buried in fine print, misrepresents the product or service, the merchandise was priced unfairly, or may be written in language you did not understand. If such is the case, you may have the debt discharged on these grounds.

Challenge a Default Judgement...

It is almost commonplace for the creditor to win a default judgement without the debtor even getting the summons to appear in court. If this happens to you, you can challenge the Default Judgement.

Write to the creditor and tell him or his lawyer you will bring legal action against them if further action is taken by them because the judgement had been obtained illegally. Send copies of the letter to the local Bar Association.

Wait out the Statue of Limitations...

If your delaying tactics have been successful, your debt may be discharged under the Statute of Limitations. The Statute of Limitations refers to a period of four, six, or eight years, depending on your state. When the debt has surpassed this time period without you making a payment, you do not have to pay because of the Statute of Limitations on a debt. Usually if you have not paid in four years, your creditor has given up the fight anyway.

SAMPLE: Out of court settlement letter

Consumer's Name
Address
City/State/Zip
Acct. #

Date

Name of Collection Manager
Name of Creditor
Street Address of Bank or Loan Company
City/State/Zip

Dear Sir:

Due to my recurring employment problem, mainly as a result of my poor health, I find it regretably out of my reach to pay my debts to your fine company. My present modest income is barely enought for me to survive on, leaving nothing for back payments. Unfortunately, I have nothing of value to sell in order to raise cash and satisfy my obligation with you or a host of other creditors in your same position.

However, I feel obligated to your company and I am willing to offer a settlement of 25¢ on the dollar as payment in full. My current balance with you is $1,425. I am able to make my $356.25 payment in full (25% of $1,425) next Friday, after I cash my paycheck.

If these terms are acceptable to you, please sign where indicated and return to me immediately.

Sincerely,
(Signature)
Name

Read, approved and accepted by: _____   _____
                                Collection Manager   Date

                                _____   _____
                                Witness   Date

Judgment Proofing
(Step by Step Process)

Because a creditor has been able to obtain a judgment on a consumer, it still does not necessarily mean that the creditor is going to be able to collect. Creditors, once they obtain a judgment, commence a process of locating property of value of the consumer's to "attach". The primary items of interest to the creditors are:

Bank Accounts – Certificates of Deposit, Savings and Checking Accounts, Money Market Funds, etc.

Income – Salary or wages made by the consumer.

Vehicles – Cars, trucks, vans; also boats and airplanes.

Real Estate – Primarily the family dwelling or any real estate with equity.

The purpose of judgment proofing is to legally protect as many/much of the consumer's assets as possible. If creditors are not able to collect on their judgment, the more apt the creditor is to giving up and going after easier "game".

Judgment proofing should be done prior to being sued. It is something the consumer should exercise whenever making a major purchase. Judgment proofing should be viewed by the consumer with the same importance and diligence as the item being purchased.

Judgment Proofing...

Step One

Find out what items are exempt in your state. All states have their own laws as to what is and what is not exempt. Even though an item may be generally exempt, it is always advisable to seek the advise of an attorney to make sure all paperwork has been executed correctly and that your rights have been asserted (Exemptions are not necessarily automatic).

Most laws (state and federal) permit the consumer to keep enough essentials (furniture, clothing, tools to a tradesman); items that prevent the consumer from becoming a public or social liability.

On a federal level, the following is a summary of what is exempt:

- Social Security trust fund payments.

- Land obtained through the Federal Homestead Laws.

- Railroad workers' pensions and benefits.

- Foreign service retirement pensions and disability funds payments.

- Central Intelligence retirement pensions and disability fund payments.

- Civil servant retirement pension and benefit fund payments.

- Veterans Administration benefits.

- Bank accounts of military personnel stationed abroad (Funds must be deposited with their branch of the service).

- Benefits to widows of U.S. Lighthouse employees.

- Benefits to workers covered by the Longshoresmans and Harborworkers Compensation Act.

Step Two

If a judgment has been obtained, the consumer should immediately reduce the balance of any bank accounts under his name. **Don't close the account;** this will only entice the creditor to keep looking. When paying bills, the consumer should do it with cashier's checks, money orders, or cash until the situation is remedied. If the consumer has not been sued and is only exercising judgment proofing as a safeguard or as a precaution for the future, he may, depending on the state, be protected if the account is jointly held. In either case, bank accounts can be quickly reduced if necessary.

Step Three

Immediately retain an attorney to homestead your home. By homesteading (depending on the state you live in) a portion, if not all of it, will be protected. Homesteading, like all judgment proofing, should be done, if possible, prior to suits.

Step Four

Attaching a consumer's wages (garnishment) is a very common and extremely effective method of collection. If the consumer is self employed or owns his own business, wage attachments can be more difficult, since he has more flexibility in wage disbursements. In some states, such as Florida, the head of household wages can be exempt, as previously explained. Always find out what laws apply in your state. If the consumer is able, he should try to receive as much of his salary in advance as possible. Remember, only current wages are attachable.

If the consumer is still unable to protect his wages with the above, there is still hope. The consumer can always file with the court for a claim of exemption. If he is able to demonstrate that he is in need of his entire wages to maintain his household, he may become exempt. Considering most people's budgets equal their wages, this task is not difficult to accomplish. Use the personal budget worksheet to demonstrate expenses as opposed to wages.

Step Five

Vehicles are also a favorite credit target for judgment satisfaction. As with other types of property, check to see if there is an exemption amount in the state law.

Also, check if the vehicle is jointly titled, and how state law affects jointly owned vehicles. Combine the exemptions amount with the amount owed (loan amount) and the current market value of the vehicle (if you do not have a Blue Book, call your local bank and tell them you may want to finance such a vehicle.) They will be more than happy to look it up for you. Another way to ascertain the true value is to look in the newspaper to see what comparable vehicles are selling for.

Example:

Fair Market Value of Vehicle	10,000
Exemption	(3,000)
Loan Amount	(5,000)
Equity	2,000

If there is substantial equity, you may consider transferring titles to a third party of your acquaintance and leasing that vehicle from him. Leased cars do not retain any equity for the lessee (consumer), and therefore are non-attachable by the creditor. You may also consider refinancing the vehicle and leaving no equity (refinancing does not necessarily have to be done by a bank or loan company. It can be done by a third party acquaintance.).

If any or a combination of the above (be resourceful and creative!) is used and the title is transferred and the vehicle is repossessed, the new owner (third party) has ten (10) days to file as a third party, and the car should be returned.

Step Six

Depending on state law, a person's marital status could be very valuable in judgment proofing even after a suit or judgment has been obtained. A husband is not necessarily responsible for his wife's previous debts, even if she chooses to transfer title to her property to him. Also, if you live in a community property state and have separate debts in you own personal name, property cannot be levied against you. (See page 90 for a list of community property states.)

As you can see, the common denominator in judgment proofing is to have use of (availability) the asset, but not ownership (at least on paper).

One important point to remember when being threatened by a creditor trying to satisfy a judgment is how much information does the creditor have on you? If it's a bank where you obtained a loan, they will surely have a credit application and a credit report on you from your original loan request, and possibly a financial or net-worth statement. This information is very useful to them and any "juggling around" of assets after the loan or suit could be contested.

CONSUMER CREDIT PROTECTION ACT

Be it enacted by the Senate and House of Representatives of the United States of America in Congress assembled, That the Consumer Credit Protection Act (15 U.S.C. 1601 et. seq.) is amended by adding at the end thereof the following new title:

"TITLE VIII – DEBT COLLECTION PRACTICES

"Sec.
"801. Short title.
"802. Findings and purpose.
"803. Definitions.
"804. Acquisition of location information.
"805. Communication in connection with debt collection.
"806. Harassment or abuse.
"807. False or misleading representations.
"808. Unfair practices.
"809. Validation of debts.
"810. Multiple debts.
"811. Legal actions by debt collectors.
"812. Furnishing certain deceptive forms.
"813. Civil liability.
"814. Administrative enforcement.
"815. Reports to Congress by the Commission.
"816. Relation to State laws.
"817. Exemption for State regulation.
"818. Effective date.

"§801. Short title

"This title may be cited as the 'Fair Debt Collection Practices Act'.

"§802. Findings and purpose

"(a) There is abundant evidence of the use of abusive, deceptive, and unfair debt collection practices by many debt collectors. Abusive debt collection practices contribute to the number of personal bankruptcies, to marital instability, to the loss of jobs, and to invasions of the individual privacy.

"(b) Existing laws and procedures for redressing these injuries are inadequate to protect consumers.

"(c) Means other than misrepresentation or other abusive debt collection practices are available for the effective collection of debts.

"(d) Abusive debt collection practices are carried on to a substantial extent in interstate commerce and through means and instrumentalities of such commerce. Even where abusive debt collection practices are purely intrastate in character, they nevertheless directly affect interstate commerce.

"(e) It is the purpose of this title to eliminate abusive debt collection practices by debt collectors, to insure that those debt collectors who refrain from using abusive debt collection practices are not competitively disadvantaged, and to promote consistent State action to protect consumers against debt collection abuses.

"§803. Definitions

"As used in this title —

"(1) The term 'Commission' means the Federal Trade Commission.

"(2) The term 'communication' means the conveying of information regarding a debt directly or indirectly to any person through any medium.

"(3) The term 'consumer' means any natural person obligated or allegedly obligated to pay any debt.

"(4) The term 'creditor' means any person who offers or extends credit creating a debt or to whom a debt is owed, but such term does not include any person to the extent that he receives an assignment or transfer of a debt in default solely for the purpose of facilitating collection of such debt for another.

"(5) The term 'debt' means any obligation or alleged obligation of a consumer to pay money arising out of a transaction in which the money, property, insurance, or services which are the subject of the transaction are primarily for personal, family, or household purposes, whether or not such obligation has been reduced to judgment.

"(6) The term 'debt collector' means any person who uses any instrumentality of interstate commerce or the mails in any business the principal purpose of which is the collection of any debts, or who regularly collects or attempts to collect, directly or indirectly, debts owed or due or asserted to be owed or due another. Notwithstanding the exclusion provided by clause (G) of the last sentence of this paragraph, the term includes any creditor who, in the process of collecting his own debts, uses any name other than his own which would indicate that a third person is collecting or attempting to collect such debts. For the purpose of section 808(6), such term also includes any person who uses any instrumentality of interstate commerce or the mails in any business the principal purpose of which is the enforcement of security interests. The term does not include —

"(A) any officer or employee of a creditor while, in the name of the creditor, collecting debts for such creditor;

"(B) any person while acting as a debt collector for another person, both of whom are related by common ownership or affiliated by corporate control, if the person acting as a debt collector does so only for persons to whom it is so related or affiliated and if the principal business of such person is not the collection of debts;

"(C) any officer or employee of the United States to the extent that collecting or attempting to collect any debt is in the performance of his official duties;

"(D) any person while serving or attempting to serve legal process on any other person in connection with the judicial enforcement of any debt;

"(E) any nonprofit organization, which, at the request of consumers, performs bona fide consumer credit counseling and assists consumers in the liquidation of their debts by receiving payments from such consumers and distributing such amounts to creditors;

"(F) any attorney-at-law collecting a debt as an attorney on behalf of and in the name of a client; and

"(G) any person collecting or attempting to collect any debt owed or due or asserted to be owed or due another to the extent such activity (i) is incidental to a bona fide fiduciary obligation or a bona fide escrow arrangement; (ii) concerns a debt which was originated by such person; (iii) concerns a debt which was not in default at the time it was obtained by such person; or (iv) concerns a debt obtained by such person as a secured party in a commercial credit transaction involving the creditor.

"(7) The term 'location information' means a consumer's place of abode and his telephone number at such place, or his place of employment.

"(8) The term 'State' means any State, territory, or possession of the United States, the District of Columbia, the Commonwealth of Puerto Rico, or any political subdivision of any of the foregoing.

"§804. Acquisition of location information

"Any debt collector communicating with any person other than the consumer for the purpose of acquiring location information about the consumer shall –

"(1) identify himself, state that he is confirming or correcting location information concerning the consumer, and, only if expressly requested, identify his employer;

"(2) not state that such consumer owes any debt;

"(3) not communicate with any such person more than once unless requested to do so by such person or unless the debt collector reasonably believes that the earlier response of such person is erroneous or incomplete and that such person now has correct or complete location information.

"(4) not communicate by post card;

"(5) not use any language or symbol on any envelope or in the contents of any communication effected by the mails or telegram that indicates that the debt collector is in the debt collection business or that the communication relates to the collection of a debt; and

"(6) after the debt collector knows the consumer is represented by an attorney with regard to the subject debt and has knowledge of, or can readily ascertain, such attorney's name and address, not communicate with any person other than that attorney, unless the attorney fails to respond within a reasonable period of time to communication from the debt collector.

"§805. *Communication in connection with debt collection*

"(a) COMMUNICATION WITH THE CONSUMER GENERALLY. – Without the prior consent of the consumer given directly to the debt collector or the express permission of a court of competent jurisdiction, a debt collector may not communicate with a consumer in connection with the collection of any debt –

"(1) at any unusual time or place or a time or place known or which should be known to be inconvenient to the consumer. In the absence of knowledge of circumstances to the contrary, a debt collector shall assume that the convenient time for communicating with a consumer is after 8 o'clock antimeridian and before 9 o'clock postmeridian, local time at the consumer's location;

"(2) if the debt collector knows the consumer is represented by an attorney with respect to such debt and has knowledge of, or can readily ascertain, such attorney's name and address, unless the attorney fails to respond within a reasonable period of time to a communication from the debt collector or unless the attorney consents to direct communication with the consumer; or

"(3) at the consumer's place of employment if the debt collector knows or has reason to know that the consumer's employer prohibits the consumer from receiving such communication.

"(b) COMMUNICATION WITH THIRD PARTIES. – Except as provided in section 804, without the prior consent of the consumer given directly to the debt collector, or the express permission of a court of competent jurisdiction, or as reasonably necessary to effectuate a postjudgment judicial remedy, a debt collector may not communicate, in connection with the collection of any debt, with any person other than the consumer, his attorney, a consumer reporting agency is otherwise permitted by law, the creditor, the attorney of the creditor, or the attorney of the debt collector.

"(c) CEASING COMMUNICATION. – If a consumer notifies a debt collector in writing that the consumer refuses to pay a debt or that the consumer wishes the debt collector to cease further communication with the consumer, the debt collector shall not communicate further with the consumer with respect to such debt, except –

"(1) to advise the consumer that the debt collector's further efforts are being terminated;

"(2) to notify the consumer that the debt collector or creditor may invoke specified remedies which are ordinarily invoked by such debt collector or creditor; or

"(3) where applicable, to notify the consumer that the debt collector intends to invoke a specified remedy.

If such notice from the consumer is made by mail, notification shall be complete upon receipt.

"(d) For the purpose of this section, the term 'consumer' includes the consumer's spouse, parent (if the consumer is a minor), guardian, executor, or administrator.

"§806. Harassment or abuse

"A debt collector may not engage in any conduct the natural consequence of which is to harass, oppress, or abuse any person in connection with the collection of a debt. Without limiting the general application of the foregoing, the following conduct is a violation of this section:

"(1) The use or threat of use of violence or other criminal means to harm the physical person, reputation, or property of any person.

"(2) The use of obscene or profane language the natural consequence of which is to abuse the hearer or reader.

"(3) The publication of a list of consumers who allegedly refuse to pay debts, except to a consumer reporting agency or to persons meeting the requirements of section 603(f) or 604(3) of this Act.

"(4) The advertisement for sale of any debt to coerce payment of the debt.

"(5) Causing a telephone to ring or engaging any person in telephone conversation repeatedly or continuously with intent to annoy, abuse, or harass any person at the called number.

"(6) Except as provided in section 804, the placement of telephone calls without meaningful disclosure of the caller's identity.

"§807. False or misleading representations

"A debt collector may not use any false, deceptive, or misleading representation or means in connection with the collection of any debt. Without limiting the general application of the foregoing, the following conduct is a violation of this section:

"(1) The false representation or implication that the debt collector is vouched for, bonded by, or affiliated with the United States or any State, including the use of any badge, uniform, or facsimile thereof.

"(2) The false representation of –

"(A) the character, amount, or legal status of any debt; or

"(B) any services rendered or compensation which may be lawfully received by any debt collector for the collection of a debt.

"(3) The false representation or implication that any individual is an attorney or that any communication is from an attorney.

"(4) The representation or implication that nonpayment of any debt will result in the arrest or imprisonment of any person or the seizure, garnishment, attachment, or sale of any property or wages of any person unless such action is lawful and the debt collector or creditor intends to take such action.

"(5) The threat to take any action that cannot legally be taken or that is not intended to be taken.

"(6) The false representation or implication that a sale, referral, or other transfer of any interest in a debt shall cause the consumer to –

"(A) lose any claim or defense to payment of the debt; or

"(B) become subject to any practice prohibited by this title.

"(7) The false representation or implication that the consumer committed any crime or other conduct in order to disgrace the consumer.

"(8) Communicating or threatening to communicate to any person credit information which is known or which should be known to be false, including the failure to communicate that a disputed debt is disputed.

"(9) The use or distribution of any written communication which simulates or is falsely represented to be a document authorized, issues, or approved by any court, official, or agency of the United States or any State, or which creates a false impression as to its source, authorization, or approval.

"(10) The use of any false representation or deceptive means to collect or attempt to collect any debt or to obtain information concerning a consumer.

"(11) Except as otherwise provided for communications to acquire location information under section 804, the failure to disclose clearly in all communications made to collect a debt or to obtain information about a consumer, that the debt collector is attempting to collect a debt and that any information obtained will be used for that purpose.

"(12) The false representation or implication that accounts have been turned over to innocent purchasers for value.

"(13) The false representation or implication that documents are legal process.

"(14) The use of any business, company, or organization name other than the true name of the debt collector's business, company, or organization.

"(15) The false representation or implication that documents are not legal process forms or do not require action by the consumer.